W9-CNB-149

stitch+ string lab

for Kids

40+ Creative Projects to Sew,
Embroider, Weave, Wrap, and Tie

- -

CASSIE STEPHENS

QUARRY

contents

4 Introduction

5 Getting Started: Creating with Fibers
   Creating a Fiber Craft Space **5**
   Preparing a Fiber Arts Kit **5**
   Fabrics and Stuffing **10**
   Felting Supplies **11**

12 The Basics
   Working with Fabric + Thread
   Cutting the Fabrics **12**
   Working with Thread and
    Embroidery Floss **13**
   Using an Embroidery Hoop **15**

16 Stitching Basics: Know Before You Sew
   Threading a Needle **16**
   Tying a Knot **17**
   Forming the Three Basic Stitches **17**
   Finishing Stitching **20**
   Sewing on a Button **20**
   Fixing a Mistake **21**

unit

1

embroidery 22

Lab 1: Embroidery Wall
    Hanging **24**
Lab 2: Beginner Embroidered
    Sun Catchers **26**
Lab 3: Running Stitch
    Tapestry **28**
Lab 4: Radial Embroidery with
    Dyed Fabric **30**
Lab 5: Appliqué Embroidery **32**
Lab 6: Needlework Sampler **34**

unit 2

unit 3

unit 4

hand sewing 38

Lab 7: Plushie Pins **40**

Lab 8: Donut Keychain or Pillow **42**

Lab 9: Gathered Flower Brooch **44**

Lab 10: Sunglasses Case **46**

Lab 11: Drawstring Bag **48**

Lab 12: Simple + Small Pillow with Tassels **50**

Lab 13: Easy Monster Stuffie **52**

Lab 14: Stitched Sketchbook Cover **54**

Lab 15: Pizza Pillows **56**

Lab 16: Scribble Monster Stuffie **58**

Lab 17: Monster Wall Pockets **60**

Lab 18: Sock Owl Pincushion **62**

Lab 19: Cat + Mouse Pincushion **64**

Lab 20: Stuffed Rainbow Cloud **68**

fiber arts 72

Lab 21: Pom Poms **74**

Lab 22: Rainbow Pom Pom Necklace **76**

Lab 23: Yarn Tassels **78**

Lab 24: Yarn Bombed Heart Wall Hanging **80**

Lab 25: Yarn Wrapped Worry Dolls **82**

Lab 26: Worry Dolls Skirts **84**

Lab 27: Touchy-Feely Tapestry **85**

Lab 28: Ojos de Dios **88**

Lab 29: String Art **90**

Lab 30: Spool Knitting **94**

Lab 31: Finger Knitting **97**

Lab 32: Wet Felted Fiber **100**

Lab 33: Needle Felted Glitter Tree **102**

Lab 34: Needle Felted Patches **104**

Lab 35: Colorful Shibori **108**

Lab 36: Marble Rolled Fabric **110**

weaving + string craft 112

Lab 37: Woven Mat **114**

Lab 38: Woven Basket **117**

Lab 39: Woven Pouch **120**

Lab 40: Circle Loom Weaving **124**

Lab 41: Picture Frame Weaving **127**

Lab 42: Tree Weaving **130**

Lab 43: Straw Weaving **134**

Lab 44: Kumihimo **138**

introduction

WHEN I WAS A KID, I didn't have art class. Instead, I attended all the vacation Bible schools that they had in Joliet, Illinois where I grew up in the 80's. It didn't matter the denomination of the church: if they had Kool-Aide and crafts, I was going to be there. It was during those summers that I learned yarn crafts like straw weaving and how to make pompoms. I also spent a lot of time with my crafty grandmother during those summers. She, like me, loved all forms of fibers arts. Her small home was filled to the brim with her embroidered pillows and wall hangings. I remember the summer I spent, sitting on her porch, embroidering my very first image of a dog at play. Once it was complete, she stitched it into a pillow for me that I cherished, with pride, for years.

Fiber arts has always resonated with me for a couple of reasons: it's tactile and, often, functional. It's all about the feel of the fabric, the softness of the yarn, the slick shiny look of embroidery floss. I also love being able to create a useable, practical object like a woven bookmark or a handmade pillow. Art that can serve a purpose beyond being a thing of beauty has always been important to me.

When I became an art teacher 20 years ago, I wanted to bring projects to my students that went beyond beautiful things to put on display. I still want to teach life skills such as sewing and weaving. I want to share my passion for fiber arts and the creation of functional objects. I want to bring back the wonderful skills that our grandmothers regularly practiced.

Through fiber arts, you can learn about history, geography, math, science, and art. In this day and age when we almost constantly have a phone in our hand, I want to teach the skills and inspiration that will make you want to set down the phone and pick up a needle and thread!

getting started: creating with fibers

FIBER ARTS ENCOMPASS every form of creating with fiber and yarn. That's a huge spectrum of sewing, embroidering, knitting, weaving, and felting fun! Because there is value in all forms of fiber arts, there's a bit of everything in this book. The labs can be accomplished in any order. However, they are presented in an order that allows readers to learn along the way and build upon knowledge previously gained.

Before starting any of the labs, it is important to carefully read this opening section, which covers all the basics about creating a fiber art space, collecting stitching tools and fiber supplies, and basic stitching techniques, to get you and your fiber art enthusiast started. For example, in many of the labs, you will need to thread a needle, the "Know Before You Sew" section provides step-by-step instructions for threading a needle, as well as how to make and use a needle threader. This section of the book should be referenced often while working through the labs. If you struggle with a lab, it might be helpful to complete preceding labs first or refresh basic knowledge.

creating a fiber craft space

It is important to establish a designated and well-organized work and storage space in which kids (and adults) can stitch, weave, and sew. Unlike painting or working with clay, working with fibers is a lot less messy, which is great for creating with kids. The space should have good lighting and a desk or kitchen or even a dining room table for children to use for stitching and creating. Some supplies, like pins and needles, are small and sharp, so it is important to provide a tray or other surface with a bit of an edge to keep needles and pins from falling off the table.

Once you establish space for your artist, you'll have fun starting a fiber-filled sewing and embroidery kit. You don't need to buy all the supplies at one time, but it's hard not to! Add to the fiber kit over time as your child develops skills and the desire to create. Creating alongside your young artist can be a wonderful opportunity for them to see you as a lifelong learner. Even if you have

never stitched before, that's okay! It will be a fun-filled fiber exploration for you both.

preparing a fiber arts kit

The best way to get started and create enthusiasm for working with fibers is to make a sewing or "fiber arts" kit. Keeping all the supplies contained within an organized box makes it easy for your artist to find, and store their sewing tools and favorite threads, floss, and yarns, and put them all away with little mess. The box itself can be something from around the house: a small clear plastic tub, a metal cookie tin, even a lunch box makes a great sewing kit. Baskets, or anything woven or with holes, are not suitable for the supplies that might fall out, but they are great for yarn and fabric. Craft and fabric stores sell a variety of sewing boxes. If younger siblings are nearby, keep the kit stored high on a shelf when no one is using it.

Let's start with a few basics that every fiber arts kit needs. Of course, you'll need a basket or shelf to store the yarn and fabric, but keeping all your supplies in one place will keep your artist organized and ready to create.

You need the basic sewing tools to get started: needles, pins, scissors, and embroidery hoops, and a selection of thread, floss, and yarn to add to the excitement.

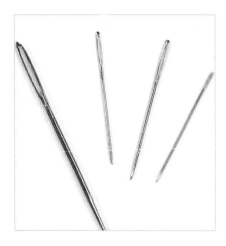

needles

There are a wide variety of sewing and embroidery needles, all slightly different to best serve specific purposes. The differences are the size of the eye for the thread to go through; the length of the needle; and the sharpness of the point. For the labs in this book, you only need chenille, embroidery, and tapestry needles.

Chenille needles for sewing

If you only purchase one kind of needle, make it a chenille needle. Chenille needles are ideal because they have a large eye, for easy threading, and a sharp point. These needles come in different sizes; the higher the number, the smaller the needle. To complete most of the labs, chenille needles sized between 18-24 are ideal.

Embroidery needles for embroidery

Embroidery needles have a smaller eye than chenille needles, which can make threading a little more difficult for young artists. However, embroidery needles are nice to have

in your fiber arts kit. They are often sold in a variety pack of different sizes between 1 and 5; the largest needle size is 1.

Tapestry needles for weaving and beginner stitching

Tapestry needles are ideal for beginning stitchers. They are a bit larger than embroidery and chenille needles, with a large eye and a blunt tip, perfect for young artists with smaller hands. Tapestry needles are found in either metal or plastic. Young artists seem to like the metal ones because they feel as though they are using the "real thing." Tapestry needles also come in different sizes. A size 13 is perfect for burlap stitching or weaving, while size 20 is great for smaller stitch work.

sewing pins + a magnetic pincushion or wand

Pins are used to temporarily hold fabric and trims in place until

stitches permanently tack them down. Like needles, there are a variety of sewing pins. You only need one kind of pin to complete the labs in this book: extra-long ball head pins. These pins are ideal for small hands. The colorful ball end makes them easier to keep track of.

No one wants to step on a pin or find a sewing needle lying around! The best way for children to avoid disasters with spilled or misplaced pins and needles is with a magnetic pincushion or magnetic wand. Both can be found at the craft store. When cleaning up, simply wave the magnet over the work area to magically pick up all the metal pins and needles.

scissors

Cutting fabric with the wrong scissors can lead to a lot of frustration. For this reason, getting three different kind of scissors for a child's sewing kit is ideal.

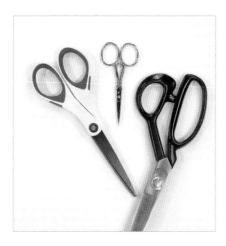

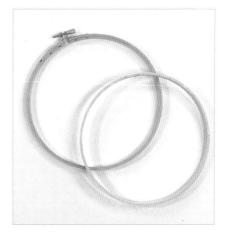

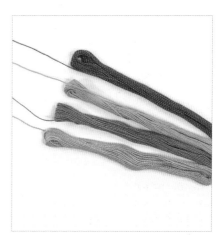

Craft scissors are basic, inexpensive scissors that can be used to cut almost anything, except perhaps fabric. They are perfect for cutting paper patterns, cardboard, and most threads.

Fabric scissors are more expensive and should only be used on fabric. You might need to remind your young artist about this many times, because it is important! Fabric scissors will dull and not work as well on fabric if they are used on paper. So, having a special pair of scissors for only cutting fabric is ideal.

Embroidery and sewing scissors are small scissors that are great for trimming small sewing threads. Their small size makes it easier to trim the threads closely.

embroidery hoops

An assortment of different size embroidery hoops is a wonderful addition to a sewing and fiber arts kit. They are inexpensive and available in plastic or wood; the wooden ones are easier for young artists to use. An embroidery hoop consists of two hoops, the outer hoop has a screw for tightening at the top and the inside hoop is a circle.

As a general rule of thumb, the fabric used in an embroidery hoop should be about 2" (5 cm) larger all around than the hoop. The hoop stretches fabric taunt, making it easier to stitch and embroider. See "Using an Embroidery Hoop" on page 15. Consider purchasing three different size hoops for variety.

thread, floss, and yarn

You only need to fill your fiber arts kit with crochet thread, embroidery floss, and yarn for your artist to create all the projects in the stitching labs.

Crochet thread is the thread used for sewing. It comes in a variety of sizes. You'll want to look for number 10. It is ideal for sewing with children because it is strong and won't break like sewing machine thread.

Craft cord is like crochet thread but thicker. It can be used in place of crochet thread if desired.

Embroidery floss is great for decorative stitching and applique. It comes in a variety of beautiful colors and is fun to use when creating a colorful image with stitches. Embroidery floss consists of six strands twisted together. Usually, artists work with three strands at a time. See "Separating Embroidery Floss" on page 14 for more information about how to work with this colorful thread.

Yarn

Yarn is used in many fiber arts. It comes in a variety of sizes, textures, and colors, although most of the yarn featured in the labs is medium thickness (size 4). For some labs, slightly thicker yarns are used. Shopping for yarn is so fun, children are often drawn to the variegated or color-changing yarns.

Yarn is typically sold in skeins, which are twisted bundles of yarn. The end of the yarn can be found on either end of the skein, but sometimes it is difficult to find and you might be tempted to unwrap the yarn from around the outside. That is fine, but can lead to tangled yarn. When shopping for yarn, look for a skein where you can see a small tail of yarn hanging from either end of the skein. When you start working with the skein, gently pull the yarn from the end.

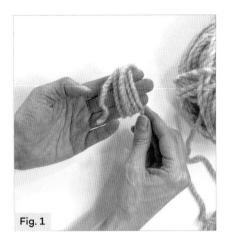

Fig. 1

Sometimes it is easier to work from a ball of yarn.

1. To turn the skein into a ball of yarn, begin by wrapping the yarn around your fingers. **(Fig. 1)**

2. Then, slide the bundle off your fingers and continue wrapping the yarn around the bundle, turning the bundle as you go. **(Fig. 2)**

3. Continue until all the yarn has been wrapped into a ball.

ball of thread wax

Some type of wax it great to have on hand if your young artist is struggling with thread or embroidery floss that is constantly knotting as they stitch.

With one finger, hold the thread against the wax and use your other hand to pull the thread against the wax. This adds a little stiffness to the floss and minimizes the knotting. Bee's wax is ideal, but even a candle can work!

Fig. 2

Fig. 3

buttons

Keep and collect a stash of buttons, in all shapes, sizes, and colors. Keep in mind that buttonholes come in different sizes, so you'll need a variety of buttons. Look for buttons with large buttonholes, these are easier to stitch onto the fabric.

glue

In many labs, there is an option to either glue or stitch pieces of fabric together. Regular "school glue" isn't strong enough to do the trick. Fabric glue is ideal. Aleene's Tacky Glue, found in craft stores, is a fantastic glue for adding fabric bits and pieces to a stitched piece.

fabrics + stuffing

You only need four different types of fabric to complete all the projects featured in the labs. Each fabric has its own unique qualities and reasons for being chosen for specific projects. See "Cutting the Fabrics" on page 12 for more information.

Starting at the top and moving clockwise, the four fabrics are:

quilter's cotton

This basic, 100% cotton fabric is easy to cut and comes in a wide variety of fun prints. The side with the print is called the "right side" while the other side is called the "wrong side". This is important to pay attention to when sewing.

In quilting shops, quilting cotton is often sold in "fat quarters" which are one-fourth of a yard cuts of fabric. This is an inexpensive way for your young artist to choose a variety of prints. This fabric is ideal for sewing and embroidery.

felt

Craft store felt is a wonderful fabric for kids; it is easy to cut and, unlike quilter's fabric, the cut edges do not fray. For that reason, craft felt is excellent for appliqué or cutting and stitching small cut pieces. It is sold by the yard and in sheets of 8" × 11" (A4) which are very inexpensive.

muslin

Muslin is an inexpensive, natural looking cotton fabric. It is just like quilter's cotton but without the print! For that reason, it is a blank canvas for stitching, printing, painting, or dying.

burlap

A great fabric for embroidery, burlap is loosely woven so artists can see through the threads as they stitch. Blunt needles can be used to stitch burlap, which makes it especially suitable for young artists, although it does fray very easily.

pillow and soft toy stuffing

To give a pillow or a plushie that soft cushiony feel, try using polyester fiber filling or poly-fil. It can be found in the sewing section of craft stores. In a pinch, however, something as inexpensive and recyclable as plastic grocery bags, work just as well. They add a nice crunch sound to a stuffed stuffie. Shredded paper, Easter grass, even bits and pieces of fabric and yarn can be used to add extra fluff to your pillow or soft toy.

felting supplies

Several labs involve two kinds of felting: needle felting and wet felting. Wool felt is great to work with because the edges don't fray like other fabrics. See labs 34, 35, and 36 for felting techniques and projects.

Wet felting occurs when wool fibers are agitated with soap and water, like what happens in a washing machine, and lock together to create a solid fabric known as wool felt.

If you've ever shrunk a wool sweater, then you've felted!

Needle felting allows you to create more detailed designs by forcing wool fibers into place with a special tool. For these labs, you need wool roving, a needle felting tool, and a needle felting cushion. Many craft stores now carry felting supplies. Be sure and see if your town has a Fiber's Guild. You might even be able to find a local alpaca or sheep farm as a source for the wool!

the basics: working with fabric + thread

cutting the fabrics

Each of the four fabrics need to be cut and prepared differently. Fabric scissors make the cutting job much easier!

cutting burlap

Burlap is loosely woven; if you look closely, you can see the strands of fiber go over and under each other, just like the projects in the weaving labs! If this fabric is cut incorrectly, it unravels, or becomes unwoven, as you work. Here's the best way to cut and prepare burlap:

1. Make a small 1" (2.5 cm) cut at one edge of the burlap. Gently separate the fabric and pull one strand of the burlap thread. **(Fig. 1)**

2. Gently continue to pull that thread all the way out of the fabric. The fabric will gather until the thread has been completely re-leased from the fabric. If the burlap strand breaks, just pull a strand of burlap beside the broken strand. **(Fig. 2)**

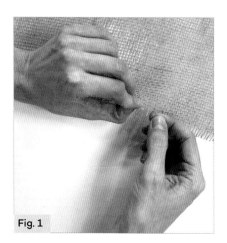
Fig. 1

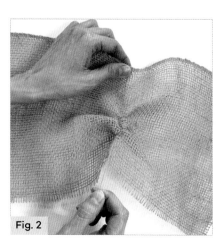
Fig. 2

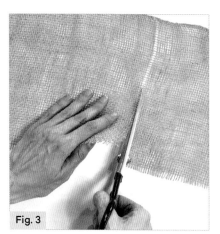
Fig. 3

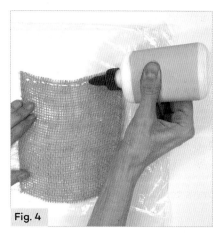
Fig. 4

3. Once the burlap strand is totally removed from the fabric, the fabric will lay flat. This creates a run or line in the fabric. Cut along this line for a straight edge in the burlap. **(Fig. 3)**

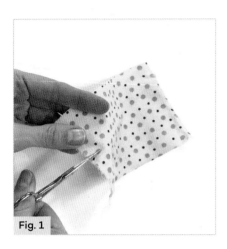

Fig. 1

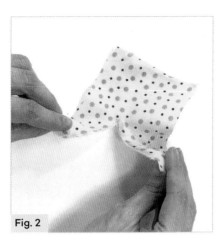

Fig. 2

4. Before stitching, draw a line of glue around the edge and allow to it dry overnight. The glue prevents the burlap from fraying during stitching. **(Fig. 4)**

cutting quilter's cotton and muslin

Quilter's cotton and muslin are both cotton fabrics and one simply features fabulous prints while the other is a solid, natural color.

1. To cut and prepare this fabric, simply make a small snip in one edge. **(Fig. 1)**

2. Gently tear the fabric to the opposite side. The fabric may have a wrinkled edge due to the tearing; press the edges flat. **(Fig. 2)**

cutting craft store felt

Craft felt is a synthetic or man-made fiber and is very inexpensive. Real felted fiber is made from wool and is much more expensive. In this book, craft felt, sold in sheets in a variety of colors, is used. This fabric doesn't ravel, so it can be cut with scissors and will either be glued or stitched to other pieces of fabric.

working with thread and embroidery floss

There are a few tips that make working with the different threads and embroidery floss easier.

cutting the correct length thread

It is important to cut the correct length of thread. Thread that is too long tends to tangle during stitching. Thread that is too short is frustrating because you need to stop, tie off, and start again.

A good thread length is about the same as the length of your arm, approximately 12"-14" (30.5-35.6 cm). Hold the thread end in one hand, outstretch your arm, and pull the thread to your shoulder. Pinch the thread near your shoulder and pull it away to cut it. Do not cut the thread near your shoulder or your hair or clothing might be cut instead!

Once cut, crochet and craft thread are ready to sew. Embroidery floss, however needs to be separated before stitching and should never be longer than 14" (35.6 cm). See "Separating Embroidery Floss" on page 14.

separating embroidery floss

Embroidery floss is made up of six strands of thread. After the floss is cut, separate the strands in half. Sometimes, the number of strands you want to use varies, but for the projects in this book, use three strands of embroidery floss.

1. Gently, separate the ends of the strands so each one is visible. **(Fig. 1)**

2. Pull just one of the strands of floss from the bunch. Pinch and hold the remaining five strands while pulling. **(Fig. 2)**

3. As the one strand is being pulled, the remaining five will gather and may appear to tangle. Do not untangle. As soon as the piece is pulled out, the strands will untangle.

4. Continue pulling two more strands from the floss, one at a time. Once finished, there should be two sets of three strands of embroidery floss for stitching. **(Fig. 3)**

storing embroidery floss

Embroidery floss can become a tangled mess. To keep this from happening, it is a good idea to wrap embroidery floss around a bobbin. Craft stores sell bobbins, but you can easily make one from a cut piece of cardboard or a plastic card.

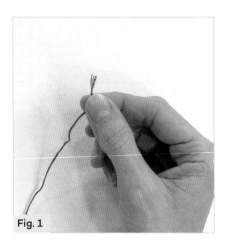
Fig. 1

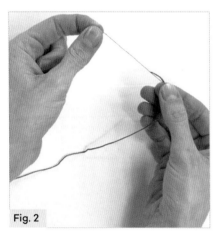
Fig. 2

Fig. 3

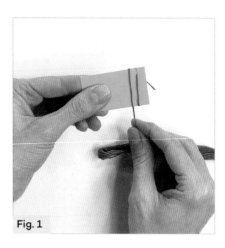
Fig. 1

Fig. 2

1. Cut a small slit on one side of a small piece of cardboard (cereal box cardboard works great). Slide the end of the floss into the slit and begin wrapping the floss around card. **(Fig. 1)**

2. Continue wrapping the floss around the card. If the floss starts to tangle, gently unravel it. To finish, cut a small slit on the opposite side of the cardboard and slide the end of the floss into it. **(Fig. 2)**

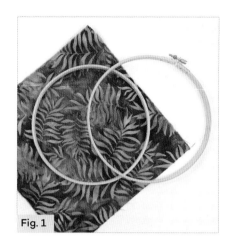

Fig. 1

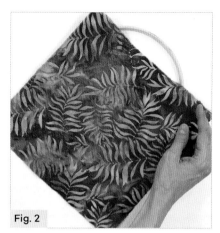

Fig. 2

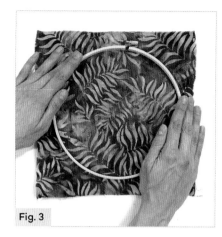

Fig. 3

using an embroidery hoop

An embroidery hoop is a wonderful tool to use when hand sewing or embroidering. It helps to hold the fabric taunt while stitching. Here is how to put fabric on an embroidery hoop:

1. Separate the hoops. **(Fig. 1)**

2. Place the circle hoop on a table. Lay the fabric over the hoop. **(Fig. 2)**

3. Place the hoop with the screw over the bottom hoop and fabric. This should be a tight fit. Either tighten or loosen the screw at the top to allow the top hoop to fit snuggly. **(Fig. 3)**

stitching basics: know before you sew

Learning to sew can be very exciting for a young artist as the possibilities of what can be created are endless. What might prove frustrating are the little things, like threading a needle, tying a knot, and untangling a mess of thread. Learning these basics make for a pleasant and successful sewing experience. For that reason, all those techniques are explained in this section. Come back to this information frequently as it is referenced often in the labs to come.

threading a needle

Threading a needle is how all sewing starts! It is the act of putting thread, yarn, or embroidery floss into the eye or the opening of the needle. If the eye is big, this can be accomplished by simply sliding the thread into the needle. Sometimes it is a bit harder to thread a needle if the eye is small. In this case, needle threaders, which can be purchased at craft stores, work wonderfully as well. However, if threading a needle is proving to be difficult and no needle threader is to be found, try making a needle threader of your own.

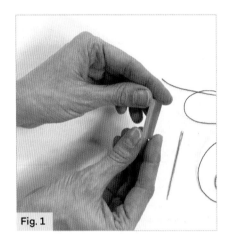
Fig. 1

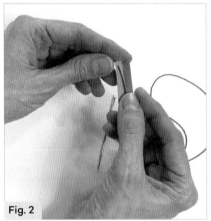
Fig. 2

making a needle threader

A homemade needle threader is free and easy to use. Here's how to make one:

1. Cut a small rectangle of paper. Fold it in half lengthwise. Make sure it is small enough to slide through the eye, or opening, of the needle. **(Fig. 1)**

2. Open the rectangle of paper. Place the end of the cut thread inside the rectangle and fold it closed. **(Fig. 2)**

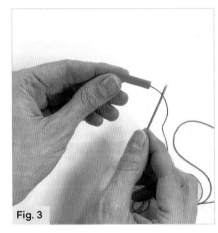
Fig. 3

3. Slide the folded rectangle with the thread inside through the eye of the needle. Take the paper off the thread and the needle is threaded. **(Fig. 3)**

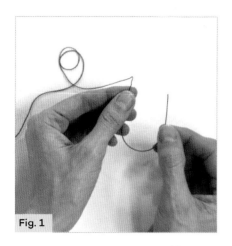

Fig. 1

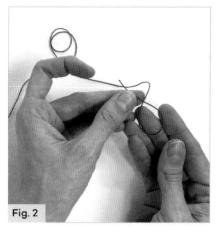

Fig. 2

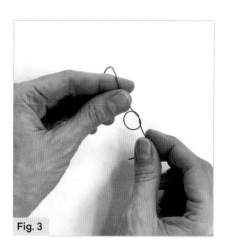

Fig. 3

tying a knot

Tying a knot at the end of the thread anchors the thread in place while stitching. Without a knot, the needle and thread simply goes through the fabric and right out!

Tie a knot at one end of the thread every time the needle is threaded. Tying a knot at the top of the needle is not a good idea because the knot will keep the needle from going through the fabric.

1. Once the needle is threaded, make a U shape with the one end of the thread. **(Fig. 1)**

2. Create an O with the thread by bringing the bottom of the thread over the top of the U. **(Fig. 2)**
3. Wrap the end of the thread around and into the O and pull. Pull slowly and try to slide the knot down to the bottom of the thread. **(Fig. 3)**

forming the three basic stitches

When doing any kind of sewing or embroidery, always begin on the back of the fabric. Thread the needle, knot the thread, place the needle behind the fabric, poke the needle through the fabric, and pull until the knot stops the thread from going any further. This keeps all the knots are on the backside of the project so they are not visible.

For sewing and embroidery, there are three basic stitches, the running stitch, the whipstitch, and the blanket stitch, that are used the most in this book. Each is different and each serves a purpose. Lab 6, Needlework Sampler (see page 34), demonstrates several additional stitches and is a perfect lab for learning more about decorative stitching.

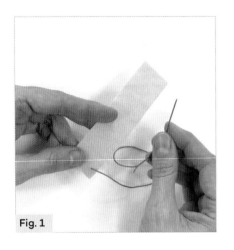

Fig. 1

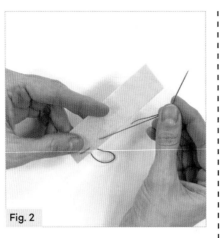

Fig. 2

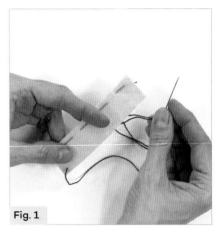

Fig. 1

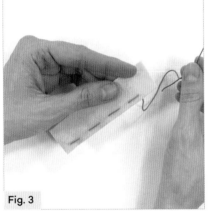

Fig. 3

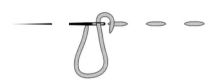

running stitch

The running stitch is the most commonly used stitch. It is a stitch created by moving the needle up-and-down, and in-and-out of the fabric. The result should look like a dashed line.

1. Thread the needle and knot the thread end. Start on the back of the fabric. Push the needle through the fabric and pull it until the knot stops the needle from going any further. **(Fig. 1)**

2. The needle is now above the fabric. Bring it back down into the fabric about a finger's width away from where it came up. Pull until the knot stops the needle. This is the first running stitch. **(Fig. 2)**

3. Continue bringing the needle up and down, creating a dashed line of running stitches. Try to keep the stitches even and straight. **(Fig. 3)**

whipstitch

Whipstitches encase the fabric edge. The needle goes around the fabric edge, not up and down like the running stitch. It is a great stitch for sewing pillows and stuffed objects as the small and close stitches keep the stuffing fiber from falling out.

1. Like the running stitch, start by threading the needle and knotting the thread end. Begin on the back of the fabric and push the needle through until the knot stops it. **(Fig. 1)**

2. Once the needle has been pulled up, bring the needle around to the back of the fabric, around the fabric edge, and pull the needle through to the top of the fabric again. **(Fig. 2)**

3. Continue bringing the needle around the fabric and up to create the stitches. **(Fig. 3)**

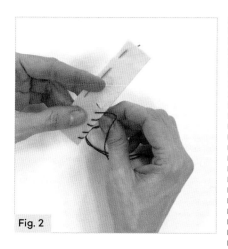
Fig. 2

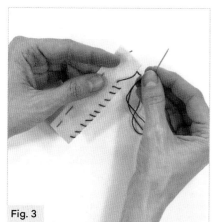
Fig. 3

blanket stitch

A blanket stitch is another common stitch. It is often used to finish the edge of a piece and create a pretty look.

1. As with all stitching, begin in the back and pull the needle up until the knot stops the thread. **(Fig. 1)**

2. Bring the needle to the back of the fabric again, about a finger's width away from the last stitch. **(Fig. 2)**

3. Pull the needle slowly. A small loop of thread should appear. Slide the needle though the loop. **(Fig. 3)**

4. Continue by bringing the needle up from behind the fabric and sliding it into the loop of thread to create the blanket stitch. **(Fig. 4)**

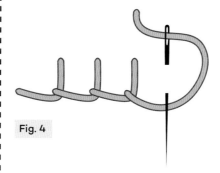
Fig. 4

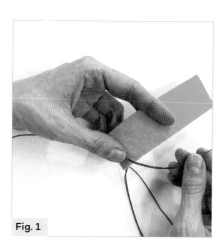
Fig. 1

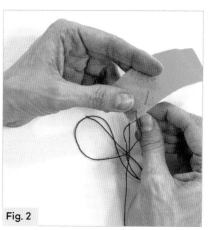
Fig. 2

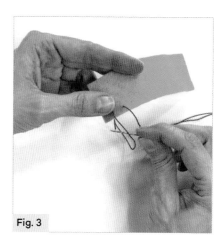
Fig. 3

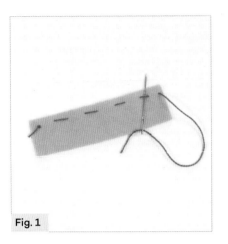

Fig. 1

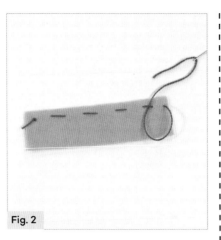

Fig. 2

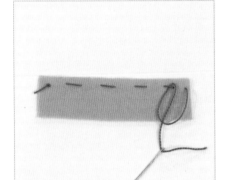

Fig. 3

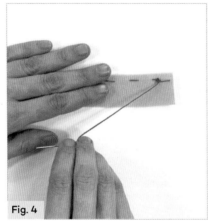

Fig. 4

3. Turn the needle around and slide it though the loop of thread. **(Fig. 3)**

4. Pull the thread tightly and repeat the steps once more to double knot the thread. **(Fig. 4)**

sewing on a button

Buttons are added to many of the projects throughout this book. Sometimes the buttons are functional and other times they are for decoration. Either way, sewing a button on is the same, each time. If there is a needlehole, make sure the needle is the correct size by sliding the needle thought the needlehole before sewing it in place.

1. Thread the needle and tie a knot to the thread end. Hold the button on the location where it will be sewn. Bring the needle up from the back of the fabric so the knot is on the back. Either slide the button

finishing stitching

A knot must always be tied to end stitching. If the thread is simply cut, then the stitches will pull out and the piece will come unsewn. This could ruin a stitched project.

A good rule of thumb, to know when it's time to knot the thread and stop stitching, is when the remaining thread is as long as your hand. Even if the line of stitching isn't finished,

it's time to knot the thread. You'll then have to cut another length of thread, rethread the needle, and continue stitching.

1. All knots are on the back of the piece. To tie a knot, turn the piece to the wrong side. Slide the needle underneath the last stitch. **(Fig. 1)**

2. Stop pulling the needle when a small loop of thread appears. **(Fig. 2)**

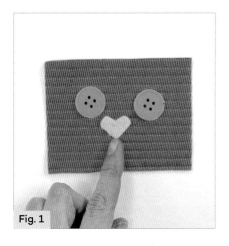

Fig. 1

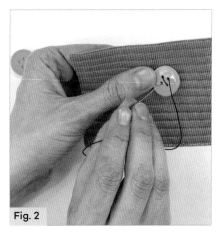

Fig. 2

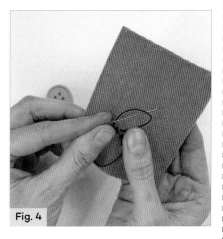

Fig. 3

Fig. 4

5. Pull the needle slowly until there is a small loop of thread remaining. Slide needle through the loop and pull. Repeat process again and then trim the extra thread. **(Fig. 6)**

fixing a mistake

In sewing, there are going to be mistakes. The easiest way to fix a mistake is to remove the thread from the needle and then, gently, use the needle to help pull the mistake stitches from the fabric.

down the needle or poke the needle up through one of the buttonholes. **(Fig. 3)**

2. Bring needle all the way up until the knot in the back of the fabric stops the needle. Now have the needle dive down into the opposite buttonhole. If the button has four holes, pick the hole that is diagonal to form an X with thread on the right side of the button. **(Fig. 4)**

3. Repeat this process for the two remaining holes in the button, if the button has four holes. If two holes, simply repeat the same sewing steps. This process can be repeated twice to really anchor the button.

4. To secure the button, turn the fabric over and knot the thread on the wrong side. To make a sewn knot, slide the needle under a stitch. **(Fig. 5)**

unit

embroidery

Embroidery is the art of decorating fabric with a needle and thread or yarn. It's different from sewing, because embroidery stitches create lines and stitch shapes that can tell a story. In every culture, embroidery can be found decorating everyday objects such as pillowcases and hand towels, as well as more decorative and festive items such as traditional garments and tapestries. In the following labs, the basic processes of selecting thread and yarn, and creating popular embroidery stitches are explored. Many of these same techniques and stitches are further explored in sewing labs found later in the book, so if you don't have a lot of experience with a needle and thread, it might make be helpful to start with some of these basic embroidery labs. Refer to the basic section (page 12) as needed.

embroidered wall hanging

In this lab, let's practice stitching with a chenille stick. Both sewing and embroidery involve pulling a needle and thread up and down through fabric. To teach our hands and mind the basics of stitching, a chenille stick can act as the needle and the thread. Try stitching through a meshlike fabric with the stick and "sewing" on a button. Have fun creating a colorful wall hanging filled with chenille stick stitches.

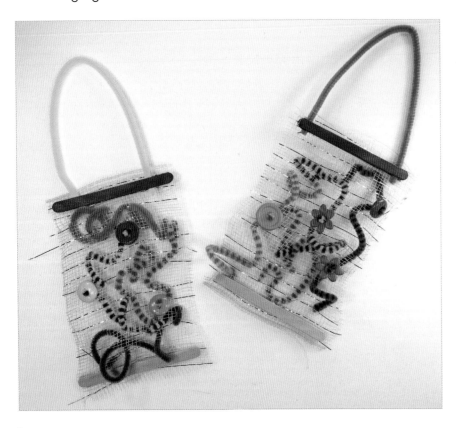

materials

→ **Floral mesh netting, 6" × 8" (15.2 × 20.3 cm)**
→ **Craft sticks**
→ **Glue**
→ **Clothespins or a heavy book**
→ **Chenille sticks**
→ **Buttons**

making the wall hanging

1. Cut a strip of the floral mesh that is as wide as the craft stick and about as long. It doesn't have to be a perfect rectangle. Place the mesh on one craft stick, draw a line of glue over the craft stick. **(Fig. 1)**

2. Add another stick directly over the first one with the mesh in between. Do the same at the opposite mesh edge, but add a hanger, by placing both ends of a chenille stick in between the two craft sticks, as shown. Hold the craft sticks together with either clothespins or a heavy book. Allow the glue to dry. **(Fig. 2)**

3. Bend the bottom of a chenille stick. This acts as a knot to anchor the chenille stick. **(Fig. 3)**

4. Starting on the back, push the chenille stick through a hole in the mesh and pull it through until the bent part at the bottom of the stick stops it. **(Fig. 4)**

5. Pull the stick up and down through the mesh. Finish stitching by pulling the stick though to the back and anchor it with a bend to hold it in place. Add as many chenille sticks as you want. **(Fig. 5)**

6. Slide a button down the stick. Bend the chenille stick and push the stick into the second hole in the button (or through the loop on the back of the button) and then push the chenille stick in and out of the mesh to anchor the button in place. Be sure to bend the ends of the stick on the back to secure the button and the stick. **(Fig. 6)**

7. Keep adding buttons and chenille sticks until your wall hanging is complete!

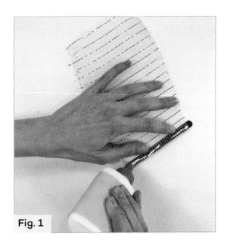

Fig. 1

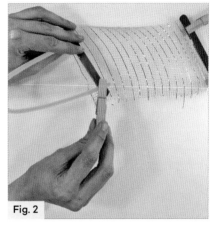

Fig. 2

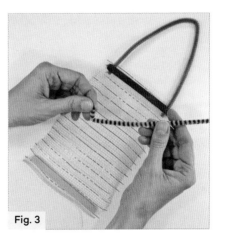

Fig. 3

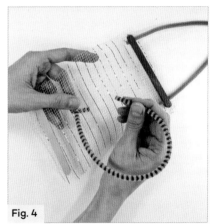

Fig. 4

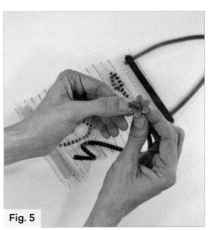

Fig. 5

Fig. 6

beginner embroidered sun catcher

Let's learn the basics of embroidery. Embroidery is creating a picture with stitches. In this lab, we explore threading a needle, using an embroidery hoop, and making stitched lines on plastic. Think of the embroidery hoop as a pond and the needle as a swimmer. The swimmer needle always jumps in and out of the pool, never around it. Have fun exploring embroidery!

materials

- → **Embroidery hoops**
- → **Clear plastic storage bags**
- → **Sharp tapestry needle**
- → **Yarn**
- → **Needle threader, optional**
- → **Pompoms, optional**

making a sun catcher

1. Separate the two embroidery hoops. Place the smaller wooden hoop on a table. Cut a square shape from a plastic bag that is larger than the embroidery hoop. Place it over the wooden hoop. Put the hoop with the screw over both the smaller hoop and the bag. If it doesn't fit, loosen the screw until it fits and then tighten the screw once it is in place. The bag should stretch tightly between the hoops. **(Fig. 1)**

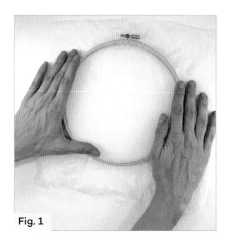

Fig. 1

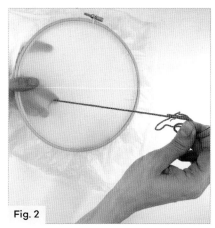

Fig. 2

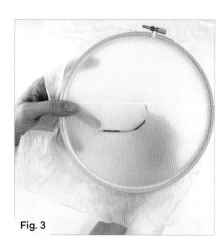

Fig. 3

2. Thread the needle with yarn. A needle threader makes threading the needle easier (see page 16). Begin stitching on the back. Poke the needle through the plastic from the back to the front and pull. Leave a small tail of yarn on the back. **(Fig. 2)** Poke the needle back down through the plastic.

3. To create embroidered stitches, pull the needle up through the plastic and then down through the plastic. **(Fig. 3)**

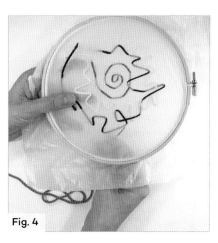

Fig. 4

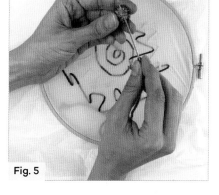

Fig. 5

tip

The needle should never go around the embroidery hoop. If it does, unthread the needle and gently pull the stitch out. Rethread the needle and continue stitching. All the stitches should take place inside the hoop.

4. When the yarn runs out, leave a small thread tail on the back. Rethread the needle and continue stitching with a new length of yarn. Try creating line designs with the stitches. **(Fig. 4)**

5. For fun, slide a pompom down the needle and thread. Add as much yarn and as many pompoms as you want. **(Fig. 5)**

6. Once you are finished, hang the embroidery hoop in a window!

running stitch tapestry

Burlap is a type of woven fabric. It's fun to embroider on because it is easy to see through while you are stitching. Try stretching burlap over an embroidery hoop or simply holding it. Let's focus on learning how to make running stitches (see page 18) and backstitches! You can add pom poms to decorate (see Lab 21).

materials

→ 6" (15.2 cm) burlap squares
→ Glue
→ Buttons
→ Yarn
→ Tapestry needle
→ Chalk
→ Scissors
→ Large craft sticks
→ Pompoms, optional
→ Embroidery hoop, optional
→ Needle threader, optional
→ Plastic bag to protect the table, optional

making the tapestry

1. Look closely at your burlap square and see how the threads weave over and under. It does unravel easily, so cover your work station with plastic, and then draw a line of glue around the edge of the burlap. Allow the glue to dry. You can stretch the burlap over an embroidery hoop if you prefer. **(Fig. 1)**

2. Thread a needle with a 12" (30.5 cm) length of yarn; using a needle threader makes it easy (see page 16). Tie a knot at one end of the yarn. (See "Stitching Basics" on page 17 for how to tie a knot.)

Always begin stitching on the back of the fabric so the knot doesn't show. Begin in a corner with one hand behind the burlap. Pull the needle up through the fabric until the knot on the back stops it.

3. Push the needle down through the fabric, leaving a small space about as wide as a finger. This is the first running stitch! (See Running stitch, page 18.) **(Fig. 2)** Continue making small running stitches around the edge of the burlap. When the yarn is as long as your hand, stop and tie a knot on the back. Rethread the needle and continue stitching around the edge. **(Fig. 3)**

4. Add a second row of running stitches. Sew on a decorative button. (See Sewing on a button, page 20.)

5. Use chalk to draw a simple design in the middle of the burlap; such as hearts, stars, initials, or rainbows. To fill these shapes in, try a backstitch. To start, sew one stitch. **(Fig. 4)** Then have your needle come up about a half inch from the last stitch, and then go back into the fabric at the first stitch. **(Fig. 5)** Tie a knot on the back when finished.

6. Glue the ends of a small length of yarn on either end of a craft stick as a hanger. Draw a line of glue along the stick and place the burlap on top. Use another craft stick with glue on it to act as the top of a sandwich. Place books on top to hold everything in place as the glue dries. **(Fig. 6)**

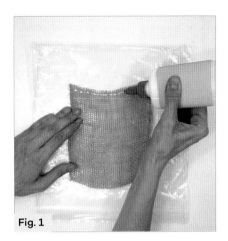
Fig. 1

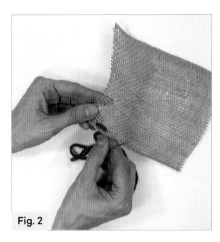
Fig. 2

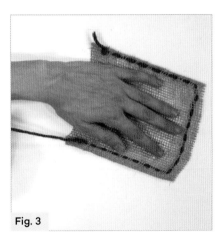
Fig. 3

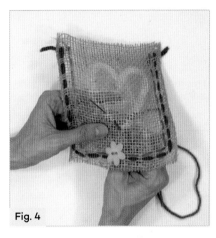
Fig. 4

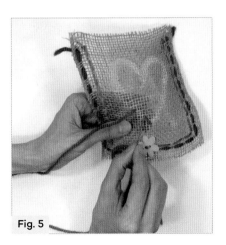
Fig. 5

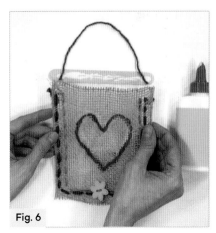
Fig. 6

radial embroidery with dyed fabric

Designing a fabric to embroider on is a lot of fun. Try experimenting with several designs on fabric before stitching. When embroidering, use the running stitch to create X's, dashed lines, and zigzags. Adding a variety of stitches makes the design unique and beautiful. See Lab 6: Embroidery Sampler, on page 34, for some decorative stitch ideas.

materials

→ Muslin, 2" (5 cm) wider all around than embroidery hoop
→ Embroidery hoop
→ Permanent markers
→ 70% alcohol
→ Paintbrush or eyedropper
→ Small dish
→ Embroidery floss
→ Embroidery needle
→ Scissors
→ Buttons

embroidering on dyed fabric

1. Stretch muslin fabric between the embroidery hoops. Use permanent markers to draw a radiating design. Start with a circle in the middle of the fabric and add lines and shapes to create a design that grows from the circle. **(Fig. 1)**

> **tip**
> You can also simply draw any colorful design with permanent markers.

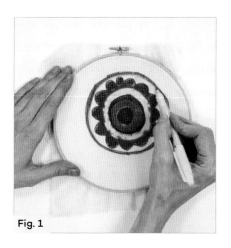
Fig. 1

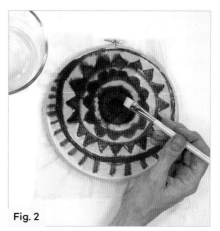
Fig. 2

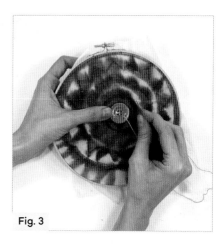
Fig. 3

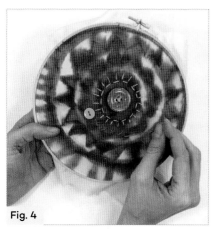
Fig. 4

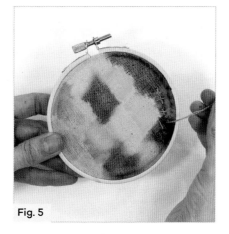
Fig. 5

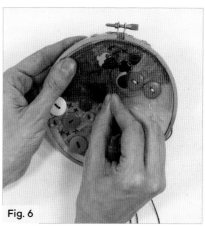
Fig. 6

2. Once the design is colored in, fill a dish with a small amount of alcohol. Use a paintbrush or a dropper to add drops of alcohol to the surface of the design. The alcohol causes the colors of the design to change and run together much like tie-dye. Let the fabric dry for at least an hour before stitching on it. **(Fig. 2)**

3. If you plan to stitch a radiating design, begin in the middle, just like you did when you drew the design.

Consider starting by stitching a button in the middle of the fabric. **(Fig. 3)**

4. Just like with the drawn design, the embroidery stitches should radiate from the center. Try using a blanket stitch, running stitch, and cross stitch to create a variety of designs. **(Fig. 4)**

5. For designs that don't radiate from the center, try exploring a

variety of stitches, like the cross stitch. **(Fig. 5)**

6. Sew on novelty buttons for a unique design. **(Fig. 6)**

tip
A cross stitch is simply two straight stitches that cross one over the other, forming an X.

appliqué embroidery

Appliqué is a technique that involves sewing a piece of fabric to other pieces of fabric to create a picture. It's like collage, but instead of using paper and glue, you use fabric, needle, and thread. In this lab, we practice appliqué using a fun print fabric for the background and cut felt shapes for the image.

materials

→ **Embroidery hoop**
→ **Printed quilter's cotton, 2" (5 cm) larger all around than embroidery hoop**
→ **Scraps of different colors of felt**
→ **Pins**
→ **Fabric scissors**
→ **Fabric marking pen or chalk**
→ **Embroidery floss**
→ **Embroidery needle**

learning to appliqué

1. Stretch the print fabric between the embroidery hoops. **(Fig. 1)**

Fig. 1

2. Draw simple shapes for an animal or any object onto felt with chalk or a fabric marker. For a perfect circle, try tracing the lid of a jar. Cut the felt with fabric scissors. Pin the shapes in place within the hoop. **(Fig. 2)**

3. Cut a length of embroidery floss 12" (30 cm). Divide the six strands of floss into half. Thread an embroidery needle with floss and knot one end of the floss. Use a running stitch to attach the felt fabric to the background. **(Fig. 3)**

4. Cut out smaller shapes for more details. Stitch these felt pieces in place with a running stitch. **(Fig. 4)**

5. Embroider designs onto the various stitched pieces. Try using different embroidery stitches (see Lab 6, page 34). **(Fig. 5)**

6. Continue adding more felt pieces and embroidery stitches until the piece is complete. **(Fig. 6)**

7. Experiment sewing different objects to an appliquéd piece, like adding a paint brush to a palette appliqué. **(Fig. 7)**

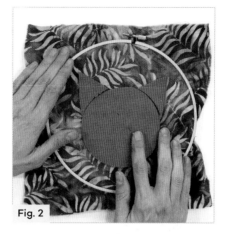
Fig. 2

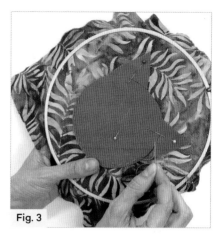
Fig. 3

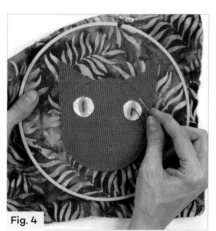
Fig. 4

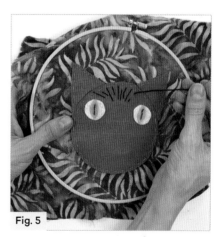
Fig. 5

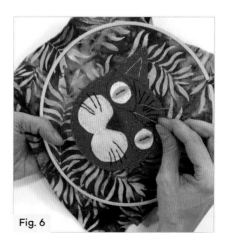
Fig. 6

Fig. 7

LAB 6
needlework sampler

Traditionally, a needlework sampler was created for an artist to show their mastery of stitches. Today, a sampler often includes an alphabet, stitched designs, and motifs. In this lab, you learn how to embroider a sampler of stitches, beyond the three basic stitches explained on page 17. This sampler can be referenced later when creating more embroidered pieces.

materials

→ Embroidery hoop
→ Muslin, 2" (5 cm) larger all around than embroidery hoop
→ Embroidery floss
→ Embroidery needle
→ Scissors
→ Chalk or pencil

making the sampler

1. Stretch the muslin between the embroidery hoops. Cut a strand of embroidery floss about 12" (30 cm) long. Separate the six embroidery floss strands in half. Thread an embroidery needle and knot the thread at one end. Begin with a couple rows of **running stitches** (see Running Stitch, page 18). **(Fig. 1)**

2. A running stitch looks like a broken line, while the **backstitch** resembles a solid line. Draw a wavy line on the muslin with chalk. Stitch a line with backstitches (See Lab 3, page 28). Continue backstitching a couple rows of stitched solid lines. **(Fig. 2)**

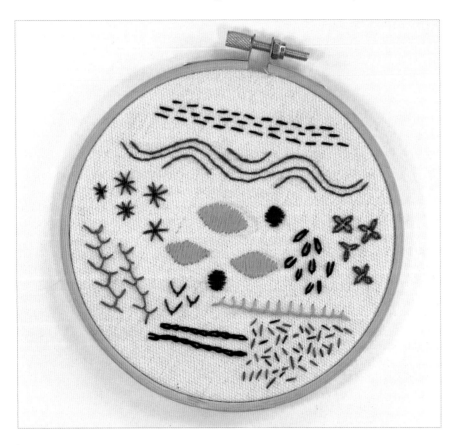

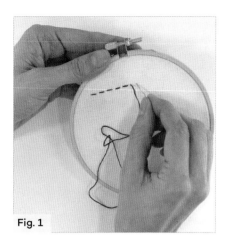

Fig. 1

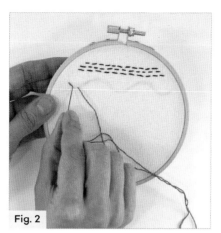

Fig. 2

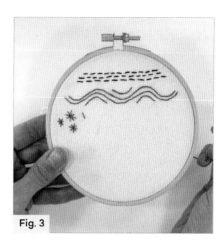

Fig. 3

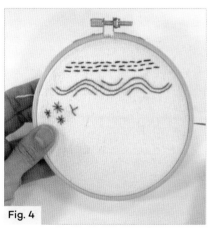

Fig. 4

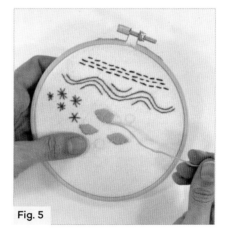

Fig. 5

3. To embroider an **asterisk**, use a pencil to mark a small dot on the fabric. This dot is the center of the asterisk.

- Starting at that dot, make a small stitch outward. **(Fig. 3)**
- Bring the needle back up through the pencil dot and make another small stitch away from the center. **(Fig. 4)**
- Continue making small stitches away from the center eight times or until you have a star or asterisk design.

4. A **satin stitch** fills a stitched space with color. The stitches lie next to each other with no spaces in between. To create a series of satin stitches, draw a simple shape like a leaf or a circle on the fabric with a fabric marker or chalk. Starting in the back, bring the needle to the right side and begin stitching at the bottom of the design, forming a straight stitch that reaches the top of the design. Continue filling in the shape with close parallel stitches. **(Fig. 5)**

(continued)

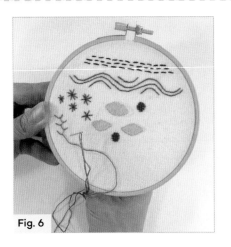

Fig. 6

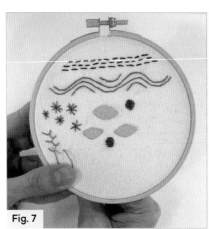

Fig. 7

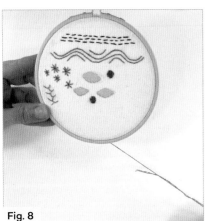

Fig. 8

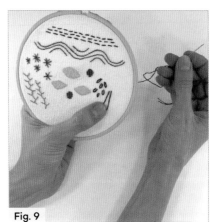

Fig. 9

5. A **featherstitch** is fun to make and adds beauty to an embroidered design.

- Begin by making a small straight stitch on the right side. **(Fig. 6)**
- Before pulling the stitch all the way through, use your thumb to pull the thread back. Poke the needle up at the middle of the stitch **(Fig. 7)**
- Finish the stitch by pulling the thread in the opposite direction of the first stitch. **(Fig. 8)**
- Repeat the process of holding the stitch, bringing the needle up the middle of that stitched space, and stitching in the opposite direction until you have a line of featherstitches.

6. To create a **flower petal stitch**, make a small straight stitch on the right side of the fabric. Use your thumb to hold the thread and add a second, very small stitch in the middle of the thread loop, directly above your thumb, and then finish pulling the initial stitch through to the wrong side. This makes a petal-like shape. Stitch a group of petals to make a flower! **(Fig. 9)**

7. A **fly stitch** is formed much like the flower petal stitch except that the initial stitch is longer, so the finished stitch is much more open and looks more like the "wings" of a fly. **(Fig. 10)**

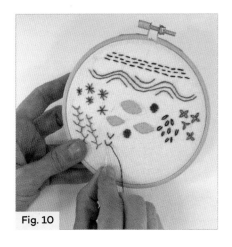

Fig. 10

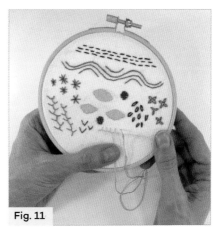

Fig. 11

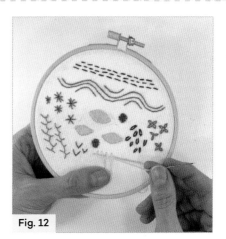

Fig. 12

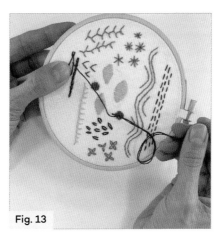

Fig. 13

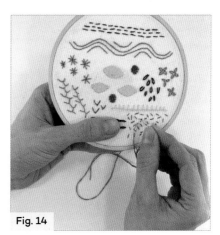

Fig. 14

8. Add a **blanket stitch** (see Blanket Stitch, page 19) to your sampler.

- You might want to start by drawing a line of chalk on the fabric. Form the stitches so they begin on the chalked line and end just above and over the line. **(Fig. 11 and Fig. 12)**

9. A **chain stitch** is very similar to a flower petal stitch, however the stitches are connected, creating a chain. Begin by forming a flower petal stitch. Bring the needle up in the middle of the stitch above where your thumb is holding the thread. Gently pull the thread, and reinsert the needle over the bottom of the stitch. This tacks the first link of the chain down. Continue forming linked stitches. **(Fig. 13)**

10. A **seed stitch** is one of the easiest stitches to make. Simply make small, straight and random stitches around the fabric. They should look like little pieces of thrown confetti! **(Fig. 14)**

unit 2

hand sewing

Sewing is the act of stitching one piece of fabric to another. Think of it like collage, but instead of attaching pieces of paper together with glue, you use stitches to hold pieces of fabric in place. When one piece of fabric is sewn on top of another to create a fabric picture, it is called appliqué. When two pieces of fabric are joined with stitches and the piece is stuffed to make a pillow or transformed into a functional holder like a pouch, then that is sewing. Many of the techniques and stitches used in embroidery are also used in sewing. Since you have learned the basics of embroidery, sewing will be a snap! Refer to stitching basics (page 16) as needed.

plushie pins

Like embroidery, there are different kind of sewing stitches. Each stitch has its own look and a different reason for being used. To make the plushie pins in this lab, you will use three stitches, the running stitch, whipstitch, and blanket stitch. Be sure to refer to Forming the Three Basic Stitches on page 17, for a refresher on how to make these stitches.

refer to Forming the Three Basic Stitches on page 17

materials

→ Scraps of different color craft felt
→ Assorted sizes of jar lids
→ Marker
→ Scissors
→ Safety pins
→ Chenille needle
→ Crochet thread
→ Pins
→ Stuffing
→ Tacky Glue
→ Assortment of buttons

1. Trace around the lid of a jar onto several different color pieces of felt with a marker. Cut out the traced circles. **(Fig. 1)**

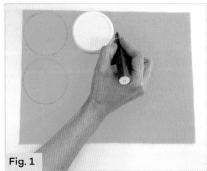

Fig. 1

2. Pin two circles together. Thread the needle and secure one end of the thread with a knot. Stitch around the edge of the two circles with a running stitch. When there is about a 1" (2.5 cm) opening, anchor the thread to the fabric with a knot. **(Fig. 2)**

3. Insert small pieces of stuffing into the opening. Once the circles are nice and soft and plump, stitch the opening closed. **(Fig. 3)**

4. Make more plushies using a whipstitch or blanket stitch to sew the circles together. **(Fig. 4 and Fig. 5)**

5. Decorate your plushies! Sew a collage of buttons, or glue small felt shapes, to one side of the plushie. **(Fig. 6)**

6. To make a plushie into a pin, open a safety pin and lay it on the back of the plushie. Cut a small strip of felt and glue it over the closed side of the pin. Allow the glue to dry before wearing your plushie pin. **(Fig. 7)**

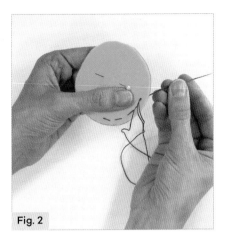

Fig. 2

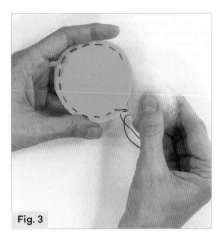

Fig. 3

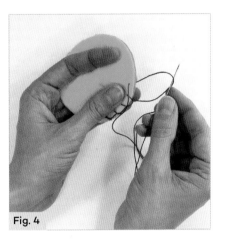

Fig. 4

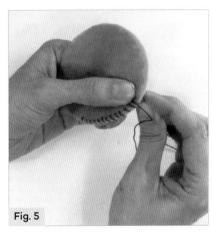

Fig. 5

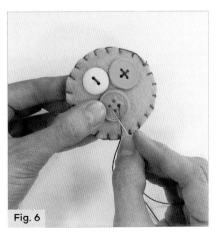

Fig. 6

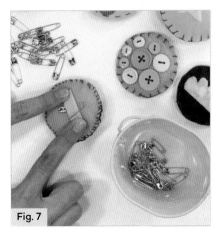

Fig. 7

donut keychain and pillow

Time to make the donuts! In this lab, try creating donuts in a variety of sizes while improving your hand sewing skills. To create a keychain donut to attach to a backpack, trace a small circle, like a lid. For a larger, pillow-sized donut, trace a dinner plate.

materials

→ Craft felt, large enough to cut out two circular shapes
→ Second sheet of craft felt for the icing
→ Scissors
→ Plate or round lid to trace
→ Pillow stuffing
→ Chenille needle
→ Crochet thread
→ Pins
→ Puffy paint (optional)

making the donut keychain and pillow

1. Trace two circles on felt. For a big donut pillow, trace a dinner plate. For a smaller one, try tracing the lid of a jar. Cut out two circles. Pin the circles together. **(Fig. 1)**

2. Thread the needle and secure one end with a knot. Use a whipstitch (see page 18) to sew the two fabric pieces together. Leave a 4" (10 cm) opening and anchor the thread to the fabric with a knot. **(Fig. 2)**

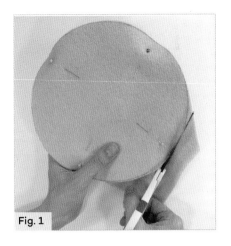

Fig. 1

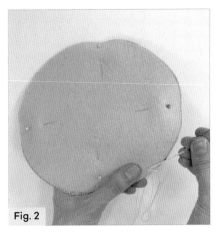

Fig. 2

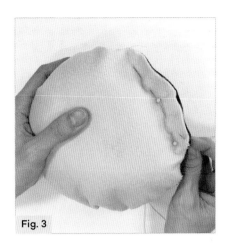

Fig. 3

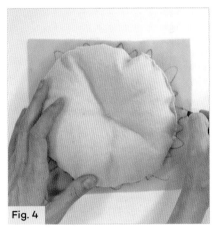

Fig. 4

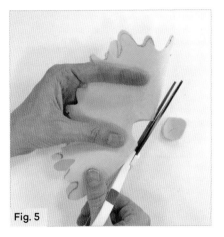

Fig. 5

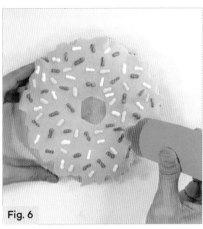

Fig. 6

3. Turn the pillow inside out to hide the stitches inside the pillow. Fill the pillow with stuffing. Pin the opening closed. Sew the opening closed with a whipstitch. **(Fig. 3)**

4. To make the "hole" in the donut, sew several straight stitches in the middle of the pillow to pull the front and the back of the pillow together.

5. Place the donut on a different color felt and trace around it with a wavy line to create the icing. **(Fig. 4)**

6. Cut the icing fabric around the wavy line. To make the hole in the middle, fold the fabric in half. Make a small snip with scissors to create an opening for the scissors to slide into. Cut out a circle. **(Fig. 5)**

7. Glue the icing to the top of the donut. Make a variety of donuts in different sizes. Use puffy paint to add texture and color. **(Fig. 6)**

or try this
To make the donut a keychain, cut a 1" × 4" (2.5 × 10.2 cm) piece for a hanging loop. Fold the loop in half and stitch it to the side of your donut.

LAB 9

gathered flower brooch

Sometimes a stitch can be used to change the shape of fabric. A gathering stitch gathers or shortens a length of fabric. It is often used in clothing like when a full skirt is gathered, or made smaller, at the waist. In this lab, a long running stitch is used as a gathering stitch to create a flower. Finish the flower with a pin on the back and wear it as a brooch or stitch it to the eyeglasses case you'll make in Lab 10 (see page 48).

materials

→ 2" × 8" (5 × 20.3 cm) strip of craft felt
→ Thread
→ Chenille needle
→ Scissors
→ Buttons

making a flower brooch

1. Cut a 12" (30 cm) long strand of thread. Thread the needle and secure one end with a knot.

2. Starting at one corner of the fabric, bring the needle all the way up until the knot stops the thread. **(Fig. 1)**

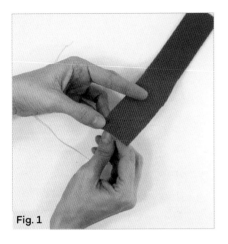

Fig. 1

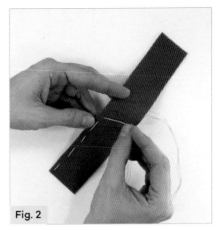

Fig. 2

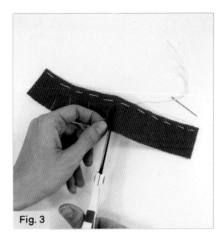

Fig. 3

Fig. 4

Fig. 5

Fig. 6

3. Stitch a running stitch along one long edge of the fabric. The stitches should be long and not close together. This kind of stitch is called a baste stitch. **(Fig. 2)**

4. Once the stitches reach the end of the fabric, leave the needle attached. With scissors, fringe cut the bottom of the fabric. Be sure not to cut the stitches. **(Fig. 3)**

5. Gently pull the end of the thread in the needle to gather the fabric. **(Fig. 4)**

6. Once the felt is completely gathered, it takes on the shape of a flower. Pinch the beginning and the end of the flower together. Add a whipstitch between both pieces of fabric to hold them together. Secure with a knot when finished. **(Fig. 5)**

7. Center a button on top of the flower. Starting in the back, sew the button to the flower. **(Fig. 6)**

8. To wear the flower as a brooch, anchor a safety pin with a piece of felt on the back as in Lab 7, page 41.

sunglasses case

Here is a fun way to create a small bag that can be used as a change purse, a sunglasses case, a clutch, and more! To make a variety of bags, just change the size of the main fabric piece. The trick to this bag is paying attention to where the handle is sewn. Once complete, try sewing on some of those gathered flowers from Lab 9 (see page 44).

materials

→ **Felt for sunglasses case,** 7" × 9" (17.8 × 22.9 cm)
→ **Felt for strap,** 10" × 1" (25.4 × 2.5 cm)
→ **Crochet thread**
→ **Chenille needle**
→ **Pins**
→ **Scissors**
→ **Buttons**
→ **Flowers from Lab 9, optional**

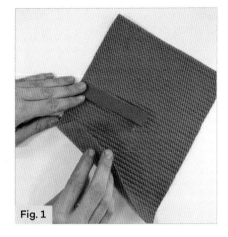

Fig. 1

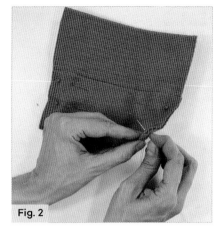

Fig. 2

making the sunglass case

1. Fold the strap in half lengthwise. Place it on the right side, long edge of the fabric, about 4" (10 cm) up from the bottom, as shown. **(Fig. 1)**

2. Fold the bottom of the fabric 3" (7.6 cm) up and pin the sides together. The strap should be sandwiched between the front and the back.

3. Thread the needle with a 12" (30 cm) length of crochet thread and knot one end. Starting at the bottom, stitch the side with a whipstitch. **(Fig. 2)**

4. Continue stitching the first side up to the top of the two layers of fabric. Anchor the thread at the top of the shorter layer with a knot. Stitch the other side in the same way. When stitching the side with the strap, be sure to stitch through both layers of the strap ends. **(Fig. 3)**

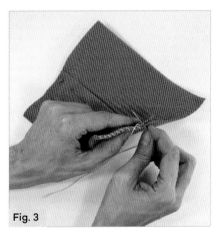

Fig. 3

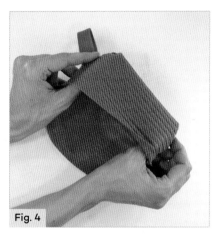

Fig. 4

5. Unpin and flip the fabric inside out. The strap should be on the outside. **(Fig. 4)**

6. To add a button, open the case. Sew a button about 1" (2.5 cm) down from the top of the opening. On the flap, cut an opening for the button hole just a little smaller than that of the button. Another option is to sew the gathered flowers created in Lab 9 (see page 44) to the flap for decoration. Now try making

clutches in different sizes for change, money, or treasures.

drawstring bag

In the previous sewing labs, you worked with craft felt which doesn't ravel. In this lab, the drawstring bag is sewn from cotton fabric. There are so many wonderful and fun prints, try picking out a couple at the craft store to sew up a variety of drawstring bags. Or create your very own fabric by following the steps in Lab 36 (see page 110). These bags are perfect from holding the worry dolls from Lab 25.

materials

→ **Fabric cut to 6" × 8"** **(15.2 × 20.3 cm)**
→ **12" (30 cm) length of yarn**
→ **Chenille needle**
→ **Embroidery floss or thread**
→ **Scissors**

making a drawstring bag

1. Fabric has two sides. The side with the pattern, or design, is called the right side. The back of the fabric is called the wrong side. Sometimes it is hard to tell the difference between the right and wrong side, so you might want to mark the wrong side with a piece of chalk. Place the rectangle of fabric on a table with the wrong side up. Lay the yarn across the fabric about a ½" (1.3 cm) from the top. **(Fig. 1)**

2. Fold the top of the fabric down over the yarn. Pin the top edge of the fabric in place. **(Fig. 2)**

3. Cut a 12" (30 cm) length of thread or embroidery floss. Embroidery floss adds a pop of color to the bag. If

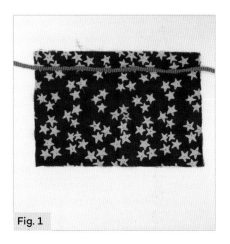
Fig. 1

Fig. 2

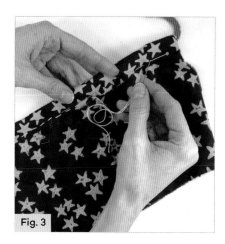
Fig. 3

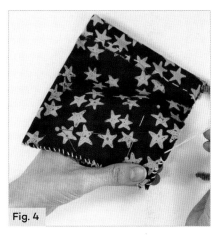
Fig. 4

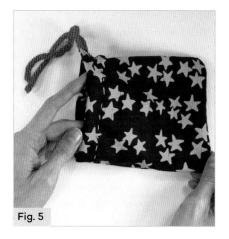
Fig. 5

Fig. 6

you use embroidery floss, divide the thread in half and slowly pull it apart (see page 13). Thread the needle and knot one end of the thread or floss. Sew the edge of the fabric in place with a running stitch across the entire length, taking care not to catch the yarn in the stitching. **(Fig. 3)**

4. Remove the pins. Fold and pin the fabric in half, with the right sides together. Whipstitch across the bottom and up the open side. **(Fig. 4)**

5. Stitch all the way to the top of the bag, stopping right under the yarn. Knot the thread to secure the stitches. Unpin and flip bag inside out. **(Fig. 5)**

6. Make an overhand knot near the end of the yarn. Pull the ends of the yarn to close the bag. If the yarn is too long, cut it. **(Fig. 6)**

LAB 12

simple + small pillow with tassels

Let's keep building sewing skills by creating a pillow with fabric instead of craft felt. Remember that printed fabric has a "right" side with the print and a "wrong" side without the print. It is important to pay attention to this before starting that first stitch. This pillow goes from simple to stupendous with a button in the middle and tassels at each corner (see Lab 23, page 78)!

(see Lab 23, page 78)

materials

→ Two 10" (25.4 cm) squares of fabric
→ Pins
→ Chenille needle
→ Crochet thread
→ Pillow stuffing
→ Button (optional)
→ Tassels (optional, see Lab 23)

making the pillow

1. Pin all four sides with right sides together. **(Fig. 1)**

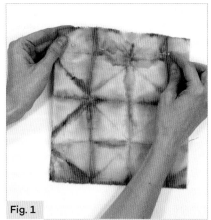

Fig. 1

2. Thread the needle and tie a knot at one end of the thread. Whipstitch the fabric pieces together on three sides. **(Fig. 2)**

3. Remove the pins and turn the pillow inside out to hide the stitches. **(Fig. 3)**

4. Stuff the pillow with as much stuffing as will fit. Make sure to stuff each corner of the pillow. Pin the open side of the pillow closed. **(Fig. 4)**

5. Whipstitch the pillow closed. **(Fig. 5)**

6. For a little added something, sew a button in the middle of the pillow. Start in the back and pull the needle through to the right side until the knot stops it. Slide the button down the needle and sew in place with a couple of stitches. See Sewing on a Button, page 20. **(Fig. 6)**

7. Make (see Lab 23) or buy four yarn tassels. Starting in the back of the pillow, pull the needle through to the right side until the knot stops it. Slide the tassel down the needle and anchor it in place with a couple of stitches. **(Fig. 7)**

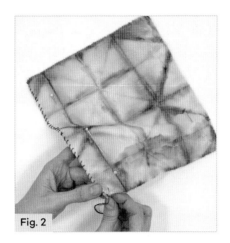

Fig. 2

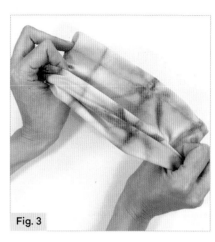

Fig. 3

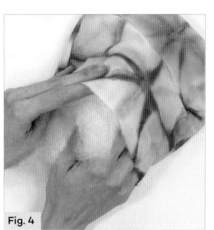

Fig. 4

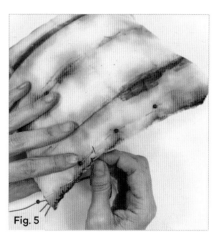

Fig. 5

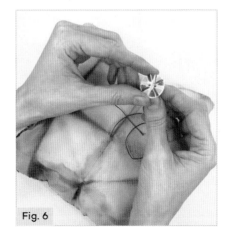

Fig. 6

Fig. 7

easy monster stuffie

Easy Monster Stuffies are just as easy to make as the pillow from Lab 12 (see page 50). You just need to add a few extra details like arms and legs; and then you can come up with the silly faces and personalities for each one!

materials

→ **One sheet of craft felt for the body**
→ **Sheets or scraps of different color craft felt for parts of body**
→ **Scissors**
→ **Pins**
→ **Chenille needles**
→ **Crochet thread**
→ **Stuffing or plastic bags**
→ **Tacky glue**

making a monster stuffie

1. Cut a sheet of craft felt in half for the front and back of the monster's body. Cut four, 2" × 2" (5 × 5 cm) strips from a different color craft felt for the arms and legs. **(Fig. 1)**

2. Place the arms and legs on the front body piece, as shown. **(Fig. 2)**

3. Pin the back body piece over the front with the arms and legs sandwiched between them; don't pin the top edge. Thread the needle and tie a knot at one end of the thread.

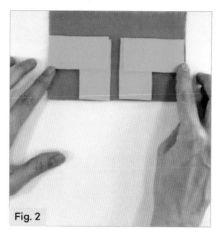

Fig. 1

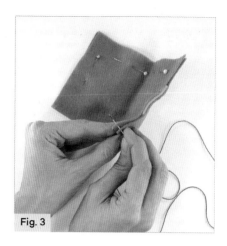

Fig. 2

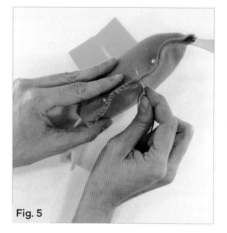

Fig. 3

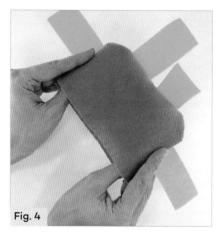

Fig. 4

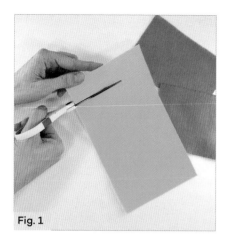

Fig. 5

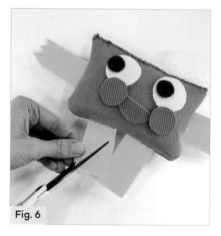

Fig. 6

Whipstitch around the sides and bottom edge; leave the top edge open. Be sure to catch the edges of the arms and legs in the stitching. **(Fig. 3)**

4. Remove the pins and turn the monster stuffie inside out. **(Fig. 4)**

5. Stuff the body; be sure to stuff the corners too. Pin the top edge closed and whipstitch across the top. **(Fig. 5)**

6. Wavy or notch cut the fingers and toes along the edges of the feet and arms. Glue features like eyes, mouths, and teeth on the front of your monster stuffie. **(Fig. 6)**

tip
Plastic bags make great stuffing!

or try this
Before sewing the monster body, try cutting and stitching the parts of the monster's face on instead using glue!

LAB 14
stitched sketchbook cover

Having a sketchbook filled with drawings is a fun way to keep track of stitching ideas. Wouldn't it be even more fun to draw in a book designed and created by you? In this lab, let's stitch a sketchbook cover!

materials

→ Small notebook
→ Chenille or sewing needle
→ Thread or split embroidery floss
→ Clothespins
→ Pins
→ Fabric, at least 2" (5 cm) larger all around than open notebook

making a sketchbook cover

1. Fold the fabric in half and place the closed notebook on top. Position it so the binding of the book lines up with the fold in the fabric, as shown. Draw a tic mark on the fabric at the top and bottom of the notebook on the open side. **(Fig. 1)**

2. Unfold the fabric. Where the tic marks are drawn, fold the top of the fabric down and the bottom up. Place the notebook on top. The fabric should now be nearly the same height as the book with about an ¼" (6 mm) at the top and the bottom. **(Fig. 2)**

Fig. 1

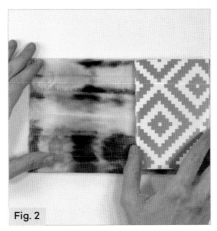

Fig. 2

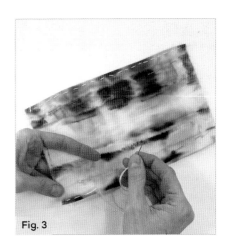

Fig. 3

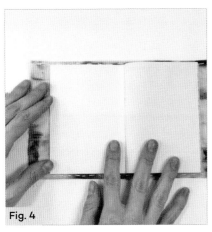

Fig. 4

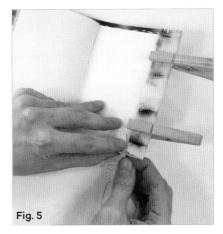

Fig. 5

3. Pin the top and bottom fabric edges together. Thread the needle and tie a knot at one end of the thread. Then, use a running stitch to stitch them together. **(Fig. 3)**

4. With the wrong side facing up, place the open notebook in the middle of the fabric. **(Fig. 4)**

5. Bring the fabric on each side over both the front and back cover of the book. Hold the fabric edges in place with clothespins. Whipstitch the overlapping fabric edges at each of the four corners. **(Fig. 5)**

or try this

Make a sketchbook or journal cover with personally designed fabric, created in either Lab 35 or 36. You can also cut out shapes and designs from felt and sew or glue them to the cover before stitching it into the book.

pizza pillows

These pizza pillows are so much fun to make and each slice can have a variety of toppings. Make enough slices to form an entire pizza. Go big with a New York style slice of pizza!

materials

→ 1 piece of brown or tan craft felt for each pizza slice
→ Felt scraps for toppings
→ Chalk
→ Scissors
→ Crochet thread
→ Chenille needle
→ Tacky glue
→ Stuffing

making a pizza pillow

1. Fold a piece of brown or tan craft felt in half from one short side to the other. The fold becomes one side of the pizza. Use chalk to draw a diagonal line starting at the bottom left corner to the opposite side, as shown. Draw a curved line like the rounded crust of a pizza back to the folded line. **(Fig. 1)**

2. Pin the felt layers together and cut along the chalk lines.

3. Cut a strand of thread about 12" (30 cm) long. Thread the needle and knot one end of the thread. Starting at the point of the pizza, whipstitch the open side of the pizza, opposite the fold, and tie a knot at the top. **(Fig. 2)**

4. So that the stitches along the side of the pizza do not show, flip the pizza inside out. Stuff the pizza pillow with craft stuffing or plastic grocery bags. The bags add a fun crunch sound to the pizza when you squeeze it. **(Fig. 3)**

5. Pin the top of the pizza closed. Whipstitch across the top of the pizza. **(Fig. 4)**

6. To add "sauce" to the pizza, lay the pizza pillow on a piece of red felt. Trace around the pizza with chalk. Then, draw a line about an inch below the curved edge, so that the sauce is slightly smaller than the pizza and allows for the crust to show. Cut out the "sauce" along the chalk lines and use glue to adhere the sauce to the pizza. **(Fig. 5)**

7. Next, it's time to cut out the toppings. Cut strips of yellow and white for the cheese; cut circles for pepperoni; and a variety of shapes to make sardines, bacon, pineapple, olives, mushrooms, and more. The pizza pillow could even have a silly face! Glue the felt shapes to the "sauce." Allow the glue to dry for an hour. **(Fig. 6)**

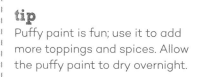

tip
Puffy paint is fun; use it to add more toppings and spices. Allow the puffy paint to dry overnight.

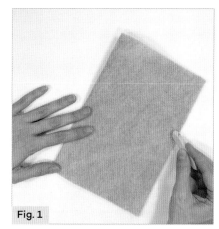

Fig. 1

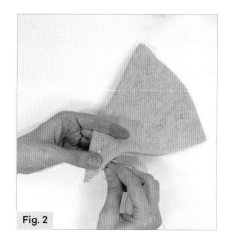

Fig. 2

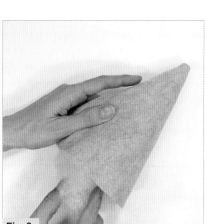

Fig. 3

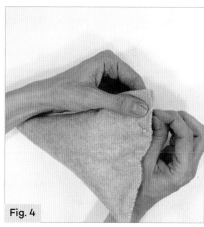

Fig. 4

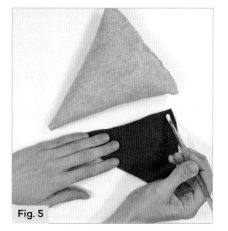

Fig. 5

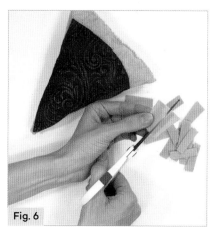

Fig. 6

scribble monster stuffie

So far, all the previous labs are made from simple shapes, like squares or circles. Now let's try creating a monster with an unusual shape. This stuffie starts with a pattern that you draw yourself!

materials

→ Paper
→ Permanent marker
→ Pins
→ Marble rolled fabric from Lab 36, enough to cut out two pattern pieces
→ Chenille needle
→ Crochet thread
→ Scissors
→ Stuffing or plastic bags
→ Felt scraps
→ Tacky Glue

making a scribble monster stuffie

1. Make the monster body pattern by drawing a circle on paper around your outstretched hand. **(Fig. 1)**

2. Sketch arms and legs extending out from the body. The arms and legs will be stuffed, so they can't be too wide or too thin. Cut around the outline of the sketch to make the pattern. Pin the pattern to both pieces of fabric and cut out the monster bodies. **(Fig. 2)**

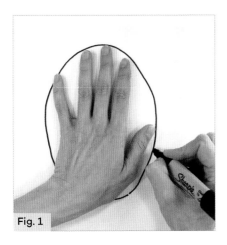

Fig. 1

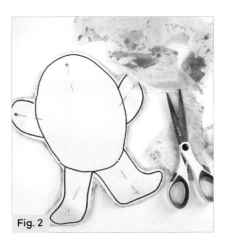

Fig. 2

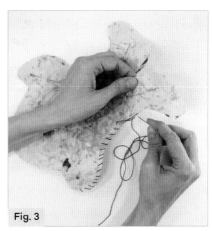

Fig. 3

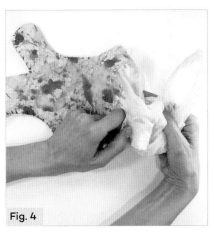

Fig. 4

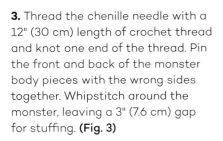

Fig. 5

3. Thread the chenille needle with a 12" (30 cm) length of crochet thread and knot one end of the thread. Pin the front and back of the monster body pieces with the wrong sides together. Whipstitch around the monster, leaving a 3" (7.6 cm) gap for stuffing. **(Fig. 3)**

4. You can stuff the monster with plastic bags or stuffing. The plastic bags will add a bit of a crunch sound when the monster is squeezed. Pin the opening closed. Whipstitch the monster closed. **(Fig. 4)**

5. Cut shapes and body parts out of felt scraps. Glue the features on the monster. The more silly the shapes, the better! **(Fig 5)**

LAB 17 monster wall pockets

Appliqué is a type of sewing where pieces of fabric are sewn onto a larger piece to form a picture or pattern. For these monster wall pockets, appliqué is used to attach circles for monster eyes and triangles for monster teeth.

materials

→ Embroidery hoops
→ Permanent marker
→ Variety of craft store felt sheets
→ Chenille needles
→ White thread
→ Scissors

making monster wall pockets

1. Trace around an embroidery hoop onto a sheet of craft felt. Trace the circle wider than the hoop by angling the marker away from the hoop. Cut out the circle. **(Fig. 1)**

2. Trace half of the hoop on the same or different color of felt to make the pocket. Again, trace wider than the hoop. Cut out the half circle. **(Fig. 2)**

3. Take the embroidery hoop apart. Place the bottom, inside hoop on a table. Lay the cut circle and the half circle on top. Loosen the screw on the top of the hoop. Place it over the bottom hoop and then tighten the screw. **(Fig. 3)**

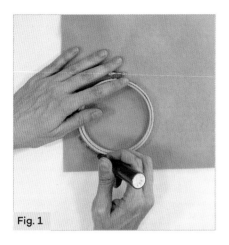

Fig. 1

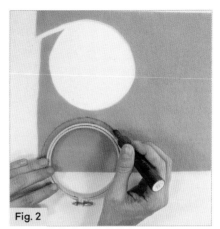

Fig. 2

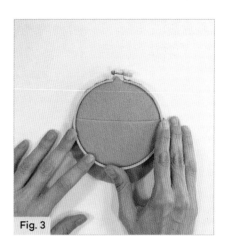

Fig. 3

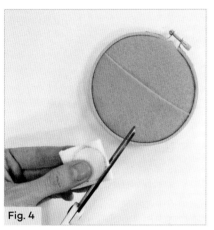

Fig. 4

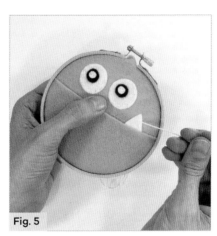

Fig. 5

4. Cut out felt shapes to make eyes, nose, and teeth. **(Fig. 4)**

5. Cut a 12" (30 cm) length of thread. Thread the needle and knot one end of the thread. Use a running stitch to sew the facial features to the monster. This type of decoration is called appliqué. **(Fig. 5)**

sock owl pincushion

LAB 18

Part of the fun of this lab is finding a sock with a cool design to use for the pincushion. This pincushion is both decorative and functional because you can use it for all your sewing projects! This means that a creation can have a job...in this case, the job is to hold pins!

materials

→ Socks
→ Scissors
→ Chenille needle
→ Crochet thread
→ Scraps of different color craft felt
→ Rice or stuffing
→ Buttons
→ Pins

making a sock owl pincushion

1. Cut a sock between the toe and the heel with an upside down 'V'. **(Fig. 1)**

2. Fill the open sock with rice or stuffing. Rice will give the sock more weight and allow it to stand up. **(Fig. 2)**

3. Cut a 12" (30 cm) length of thread. Thread the needle and knot one end of the thread. Pin the top edges together and whipstitch the top closed. **(Fig. 3)**

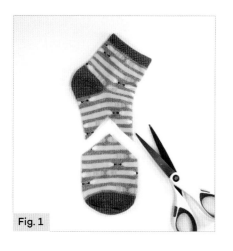

Fig. 1

Fig. 2

Fig. 3

4. Trace the shaped, sewn top of the sock onto a piece of felt. It should look like an inverted V. Draw a horizontal line between the ends of the inverted V to make a triangle. Cut out the triangle.

5. Fold down the V-shaped part of the sock. Position the long edge of the felt triangle along the folded edge of the sock. Pin everything in place and whipstitch the straight, top edge. **(Fig. 4)**

6. Sew buttons on the felt triangle, through all the layers for the owl eyes (see page 20). **(Fig. 5)**

7. Cut two wing shapes and stitch or glue them onto the owl. **(Fig. 6)**

8. Decorate the owl with puffy paint designs. **(Fig. 7)**

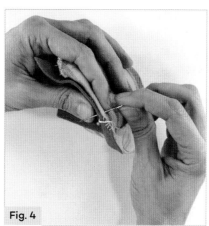

Fig. 4

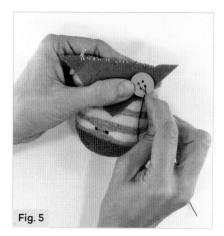

Fig. 5

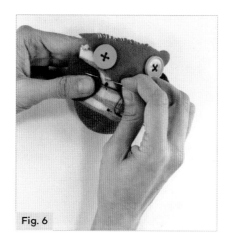

Fig. 6

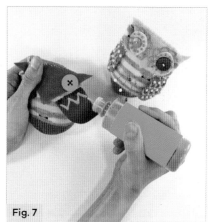

Fig. 7

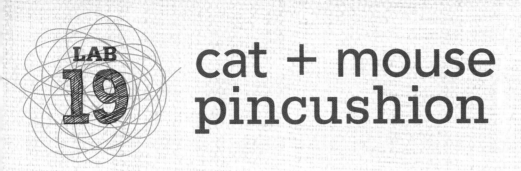

cat + mouse pincushion

Let's create a pincushion where the pins look like the whiskers of a cat...or a mouse! This lab uses a lot of the skills you learned in previous labs, from appliqué to button sewing. It's a challenge, but one that you can handle!

materials

→ Scrap of craft felt, 4 ½" × 7 ½" (11.4 × 19 cm) for each pincushion
→ Buttons, two sizes
→ Scraps of different colors of felt
→ Chenille needle
→ Crochet thread in different colors
→ Scissors
→ Rice

making a cat and mouse pincushion

1. Cut a piece of craft felt into a 4 ½" × 7 ½" (11.4 × 19 cm) rectangle. Fold it and cut in half. **(Fig. 1)**

2. Pick out buttons for the cat's eyes. Cut out a triangle or a heart shape for the cat's nose. Place the cat's features on the felt and use chalk to lightly mark their position. **(Fig. 2)**

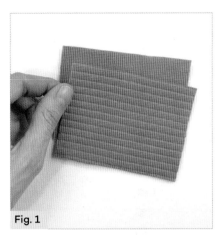

Fig. 1

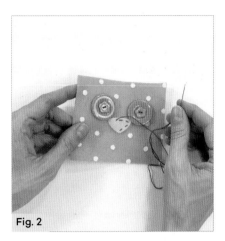

Fig. 2

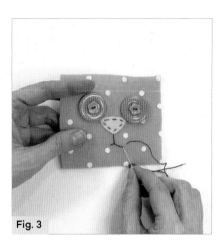

Fig. 3

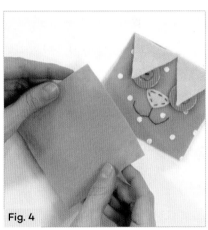

Fig. 4

Fig. 5

3. Thread the needle with a 10" (25.4 cm) length of crochet thread. Double knot the ends. Sew the larger buttons at the eye chalk markings. See Sewing on a Button, page 20.

4. Prepare the needle and thread to sew on the nose shape. Hold the nose in place. Starting in the back, bring the needle to the front. Stitch evenly spaced running stitches (see page 18) around the edges of the nose and tie a knot in the back. **(Fig. 3)**

5. Embroider the mouth with back-stitches, starting at the bottom of the nose. **(Fig. 4)**

6. Continue to backstitch the mouth lines, as shown. **(Fig. 5)** Sew the smaller buttons at the ends of the mouth lines, for the cheeks. For each ear, cut out two triangle shapes, one a bit smaller than the other. **(Fig. 6)**

(continued)

cat + mouse pincushion (continued)

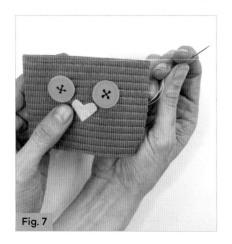

Fig. 7

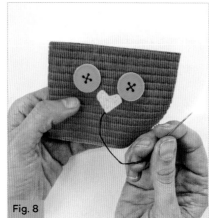

Fig. 8

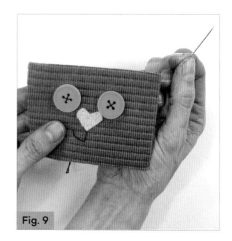

Fig. 9

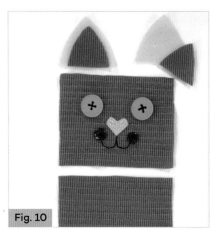

Fig. 10

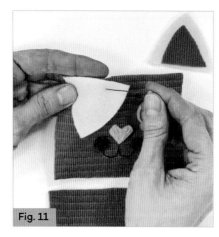

Fig. 11

7. Position the smaller ears on top of the larger ears, and then pin them, smaller ear down, as shown, on the top edge of the cat face. Cut the cat body in half along the chalked line. **(Fig. 7)**

8. Pin the two cat body pieces with the right sides together **(Fig. 8)**

9. Cut a 12" (30 cm) length of thread. Thread the needle and knot one end of the thread. Whipstitch around the sides and top of the rectangle. Leave the bottom edge open. **(Fig. 9)**

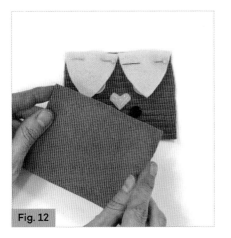

Fig. 12

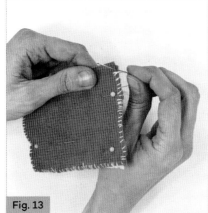

Fig. 13

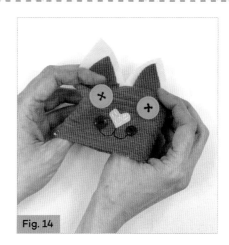

Fig. 14

10. Turn the cat body right side out. Poke out the corners so the ears are visible. **(Fig. 10)**

11. Fill the cat body with rice, leaving about an inch of room at the top. **(Fig. 11)**

12. Pin the top edges of the fabric together and whipstitch the pincushion closed. **(Fig. 12)**

Fig. 15

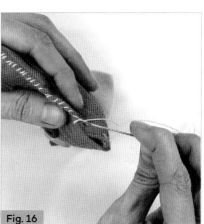

Fig. 16

or try this

For the mouse pincushion, use a small button for the mouth, eliminate the nose, round the ears, and add a tail!

stuffed rainbow cloud

When it rains, it rains rainbows! This stuffed rainbow cloud can be used as a pillow or a fun wall decoration. If you want to hang the rainbow cloud, catch the ends of a length of yarn or string in the stitching at the top edge. Hang it somewhere that needs a little happy.

materials

→ Variety of ½" (1.3 cm) -wide ribbon in rainbow colors
→ One piece of white craft felt
→ Crochet thread
→ Chenille needles
→ Scissors
→ Puffy paint (optional)
→ Buttons (optional)

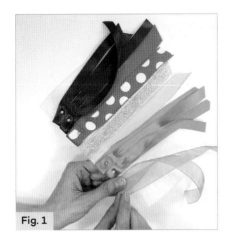
Fig. 1

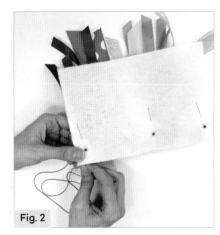
Fig. 2

making a stuffed rainbow cloud

1. Cut a piece of white craft felt in half lengthwise (short edge to short edge). Place one piece on a table horizontally. Cut between 10 and 15 lengths of colorful ribbons, each about 8" (20.3 cm) long. Pin the ribbons along the long edge of the white fabric, as shown. **(Fig. 1)**

2. Pin the remaining piece of felt on the first with the ribbons between them. Cut a 12" (30 cm) length of thread. Thread the needle and knot one end of the thread. Starting at one end of the pinned edge, whipstitch across, including both felt layers and the ends of the ribbons in the stitches. **(Fig. 2 and Fig. 3)**

3. Unpin and bring both pieces of white felt up, away from the ribbons. **(Fig. 4)**

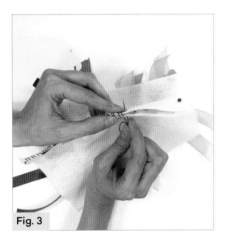
Fig. 3

Fig. 4

(continued)

Fig. 5

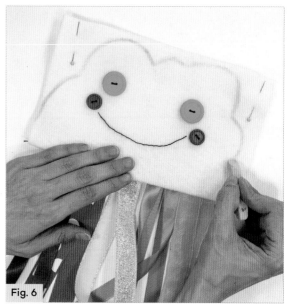

Fig. 6

4. If you want to stitch a face on the cloud, only stitch through the top layer of felt. You can use buttons for the eyes and cheeks, with a running stitched smile. **(Fig. 5)**

5. Pin the two pieces of felt together. Use a piece of chalk to draw the outline of a cloud along the sides and top edge; wavy lines look best. **(Fig. 6)**

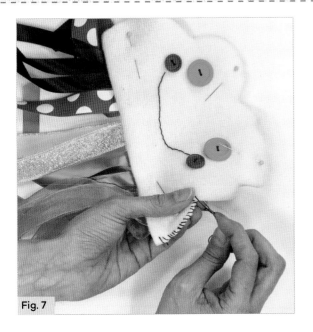
Fig. 7

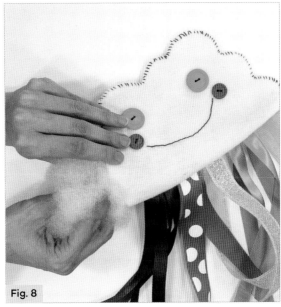
Fig. 8

6. Cut along chalk lines and repin the front and the back of the cloud together. Thread a needle with a 12" (30 cm) length of thread and knot one thread end. Starting at one end of the cloud, whipstitch the cloud nearly closed. Leave a 3" (7.6 cm) opening for the stuffing. **(Fig. 7)**

7. Stuff the cloud with pillow stuffing. Be sure to push stuffing into all curved parts of the cloud. Stitch the opening of the cloud closed. **(Fig. 8)**

or try this

Instead of buttons and stitching, you can draw the face with puffy paint, but you might want to wait to the very last step to paint the face, so you don't smear the paint.

unit

3

fiber arts

Fiber arts is just that...art created with fibers of all kinds! There are no limitations here as we explore fibers such as yarn, wool roving (or sheep's hair) and fabric in new and unusual ways which leads us to new and unusual ideas! Can a bundle of yarn be transformed into a pompom or a tassel? Can a toilet paper tube be used to create a knitting spool? Can a plain piece of fabric become a colorful work of art? With fiber arts, the answer is yes. Explore these labs with an open mind and see what amazing fiber arts masterpieces you can create!

These labs use basic sewing skills, refer to Stitching Basics: Know Before You Sew, starting on page 16, for how to thread a needle, tie a knot, form a running stitch, whipstitch, and blanket stitch, how to end a row of stitching with a knot, and how to sew on a button.

LAB
21

pom poms

Pom poms are fun and easy to make. Just grab some yarn, scissors, and a small piece of cardboard to get started. Create a collection of pom poms to make necklaces, add to fiber projects, or just to throw around like glitter!

making a pom pom

1. For a bigger pom pom, wrap the yarn around the long end of the cardboard. For a smaller pom pom, wrap the yarn around the shorter side of the cardboard. To start, hold the end of the yarn in place with your thumb. **(Fig. 1)**

2. Wrap the yarn around and around the cardboard. Be sure to overlap the yarn. The more yarn you wrap, the fluffier the pom pom.

3. When you have wrapped enough yarn, cut the end of the yarn.

4. Gently slide the yarn off the cardboard. It should look like a large letter O. If the yarn unravels, just start over again. **(Fig. 2)**

5. Cut a piece of yarn about 6" (15.2 cm) long. Place the length of yarn around the center of the wrapped yarn. **(Fig. 3)**

6. Tie a knot, pulling as tight as possible. Then tie a second knot for added security. **(Fig. 4)**

materials

→ Yarn
→ Scissors
→ 2" × 3" (5 × 7.6 cm) Cardboard

Fig. 1

Fig. 2

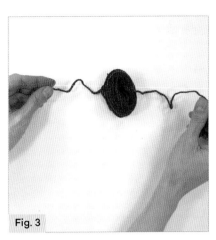

Fig. 3

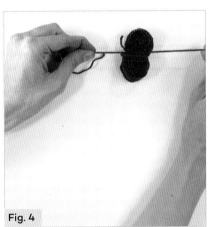

Fig. 4

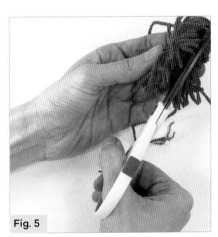

Fig. 5

Fig. 6

7. Slide the scissors under the loops on both sides of the center. Cut both the top and the bottom loops, as shown. **(Fig. 5)**

8. Now give the pom pom a haircut to make it fluffier and fuller looking. **(Fig. 6)**

rainbow pom pom necklace

With a collection of colorful pom poms, why not create a necklace? Pom pom necklaces can be made with a variety of colorful pom poms or created in rainbow order, like this one!

materials

→ Pom poms in each color of the rainbow
→ Elastic string
→ Sharp tapestry needle
→ Beads

making a pom pom necklace

1. Cut a piece of elastic string that is your favorite necklace length. For this necklace, the string is 24" (61 cm) long. Layout your pom poms in the rainbow or desired color order.

2. Thread a sharp tapestry needle with the elastic string. Find the middle of the pom pom and slide your needle through. **(Fig. 1)**

3. Continue to slide the pom poms down the needle onto the elastic string in the order of the rainbow. **(Fig. 2)**

4. Slide the pompoms to the middle of the elastic. On both sides of the pom poms, slide beads onto the string until the string is full. **(Fig. 3)**

5. Tie the ends of the elastic string together with an overhand knot. **(Fig. 4)**

Fig. 1

Fig. 2

Fig. 3

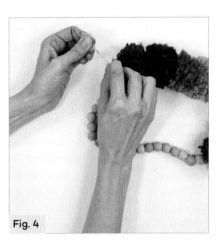

Fig. 4

yarn tassels

Like pom poms, tassels are simple to make and they are often used to decorate stitched projects (like Lab 12, see page 50). Try making some with embroidery floss for smaller tassels that can be used to make necklaces, like Lab 22 (see page 76)!

materials

→ Skein or leftover balls of yarn
→ Two 10" (25.4 cm) strands of yarn
→ Scissors
→ Cardboard, cut 2" × 3" (5 × 7.6 cm)

making a yarn tassel

1. Hold the end of yarn in place along the long edge of the cardboard. Bring the yarn to the top of the cardboard and around. **(Fig. 1)**

2. Wrap the yarn around the cardboard about fifteen to twenty times. The more it is wrapped, the fuller the tassel will be. Cut the yarn. **(Fig. 2)**

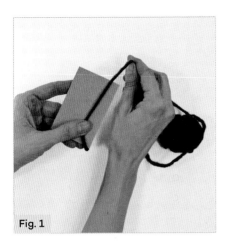

Fig. 1

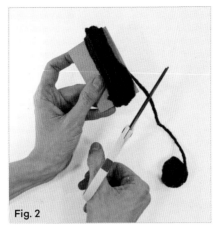

Fig. 2

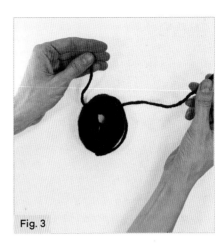

Fig. 3

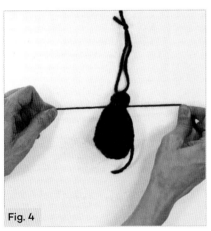

Fig. 4

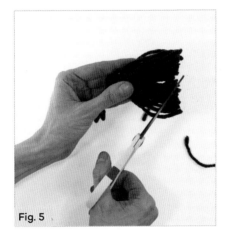

Fig. 5

3. Carefully slide the yarn off the cardboard. Gently open the yarn to see the large O-shaped opening. If the yarn unravels, just start again. At the top of the O, slide a 10" (25.4 cm) strand of yarn inside the opening. Tie the ends together with a double knot to make a hanger for the tassel. **(Fig. 3)**

4. Wrap the remaining 10" (25.4 cm) length of yarn around the O-shaped yarn about 1" (2.5 cm) from the top. Pull the 10" (25.4 cm) length of yarn tight and tie a double knot. Trim the ends of the tied yarn. **(Fig. 4)**

5. Cut through the loops at the bottom of the O to create the tassel. **(Fig. 5)**

LAB 24 yarn bombed heart wall hanging

Why not create an object to be yarn bombed? In addition to wrapping something found around the house, let's create a fun shape to wrap yarn and beads around. In this lab, let's learn to create heart shapes from chenille sticks to wrap in yarn. Once that has been mastered, explore other shapes to yarn bomb like stars, a crescent moon, even letters of the alphabet!

materials

→ Chenille sticks
→ Beads (optional)
→ Pom poms (optional)
→ Yarn, in assortment of colors and textures
→ Stick or dowel, 12" (30.5 cm) long

making a yarn bombed heart wall hanging

1. Bend a chenille stick in half. **(Fig. 1)** Bring the ends of the chenille stick toward the middle to create a heart shape. **(Fig. 2)** Overlap the ends of the stick and twist them together to form a heart. **(Fig. 3)**

2. To yarn bomb the heart, wrap the end of yarn around the chenille stick a couple of times. No need to tie a knot, the stick will hold the yarn in place. **(Fig. 4)**

Fig. 1

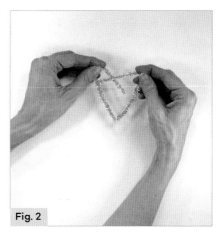

Fig. 2

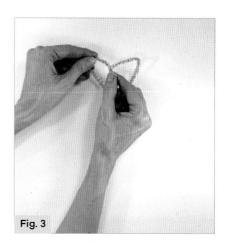

Fig. 3

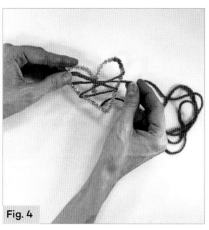

Fig. 4

Fig. 5

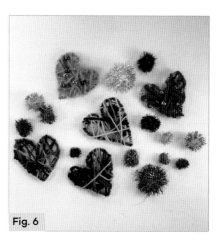

Fig. 6

3. Continue to wrap the yarn around the heart a couple of times to decorate the chenille stick. Be sure to maintain the heart shape. Add beads, if you want to, by sliding them onto the yarn; they add sparkle! **(Fig. 5)**

4. You can also slide some small pom poms into the heart and wrap the yarn around them to hold them in place. **(Fig. 6)**

5. To create a wall hanging, wrap a stick or a dowel rod with yarn. Glue the ends of the yarn in place. Then, use different length strands of yarn to tie the hearts to the stick. Add a length of yarn at the top to hang your heart art. **(Fig. 7)**

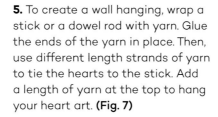

Fig. 7

yarn wrapped worry doll

Worry dolls are traditionally small, hand-made dolls from Guatemala. They are created from wire, wool, and fabric scraps. Worry dolls are usually shared with children who tell the doll their fears or worries. The doll is then placed under the child's pillow and slept on. It's believed that by morning, the doll will have taken away the worries. In this lab, worry dolls are created in a nontraditional way with clothespins and yarn.

materials

→ Wooden clothespins
→ Yarn, assorted colors and lengths
→ Chenille sticks
→ Fabric
→ Tacky glue
→ Tapestry needle (optional)
→ Permanent markers

making a yarn wrapped worry doll

1. Cut a chenille stick in half for the arms. Hold the middle of the chenille stick to the middle of the clothespin. Bring the stick around the front of the clothespin and twist into place. **(Fig. 1)**

2. The top of the clothespin is the head of the worry doll. Double knot the yarn you plan to use for the doll's torso underneath the head of the worry doll. **(Fig. 2)**

3. Wrap the yarn around the clothespin down to the chenille stick. Then make an X with the yarn, looping the yarn around the stick. Wrap the yarn all the way down one "arm" of the chenille stick to the end and back. Repeat to wrap the other "arm." Continue wrapping until the yarn reaches the waist of the worry doll. **(Fig. 3)**

4. Cut the yarn. Place a drop of tacky glue at the end of the yarn and hold it in place for thirty seconds. Or thread the yarn through a tapestry needle and slide the needle under some of the wrapped yarn to secure it. **(Fig. 4)**

5. To make pants for the worry doll, double knot a new color of yarn to the waist of the doll. Wrap yarn down one leg. Cut the yarn and glue the end or use a needle to secure the yarn end under the wrapped yarns. Repeat for the other pant leg. **(Fig. 5)**

6. To create the hair, apply glue to the top of the clothespin. Cut strands of yarn and position them on the top. Hold the yarn in place for thirty seconds. Add a face with fine tipped permanent markers, scraps of yarn for a scarf, or small pom poms for buttons. **(Fig. 6)**

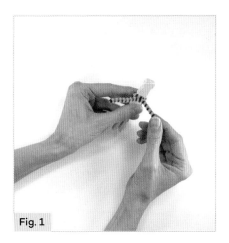

Fig. 1

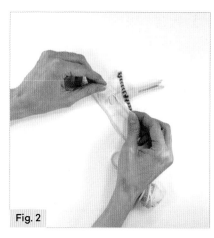

Fig. 2

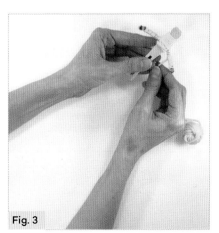

Fig. 3

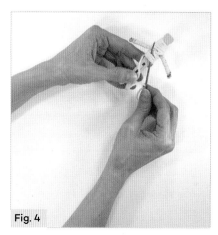

Fig. 4

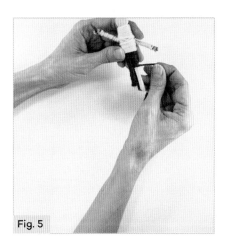

Fig. 5

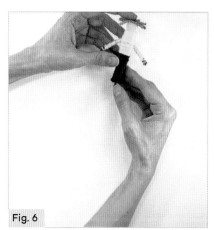

Fig. 6

worry doll skirts

Let's use some fabric scrap to make a worry doll skirt.

materials

→ Wooden clothespin
→ Yarn
→ Chenille stick
→ Fabric scrap for the skirt
→ Tacky glue
→ Tapestry needle (optional)
→ Permanent markers
→ Chenille needle
→ Thread

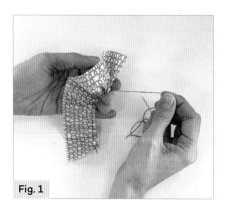

Fig. 1

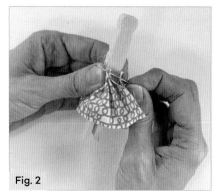

Fig. 2

making a fabric skirt for your worry doll

1. To make a fabric skirt for your worry doll, cut a strip of scrap fabric 8" × 2" (20.3 × 5 cm). Follow the baste stitch instructions, steps 1-3 in Lab 9, page 44. **(Fig. 1)**

2. Place the little skirt around the middle of the clothespin and pull the baste stitches tight and double knot them to hold the top of the skirt to the worry doll. Whipstitch the narrow edges of the skirt together from the top of the skirt to the bottom. Knot the knot the thread to hold the skirt in place. **(Fig. 2)**

Fig. 3

Fig. 4

3. Follow steps 1-4 from Lab 25, page 82 to add chenille stick arms to the clothespin and wrap yarn around the body and arms. **(Fig. 3)**

4. Glue on yarn for hair, pom poms for hats and buttons, and use markers to add shoes and face! **(Fig. 4)**

touchy-feely tapestry

A tapestry is a work of art created from fiber that is displayed on the wall. During medieval times, tapestries were woven pictures of scenes from everyday life or illustrations of fables. In this lab, the tapestry is one of yarn and color. Try adding pom poms created in Lab 21 (see page 74) for extra texture and fun.

materials

- → Stick, about 12" (30 cm) long
- → Sandpaper (optional)
- → Variety of different yarn cut into 20" (50.8 cm) lengths
- → Scissors
- → Tape

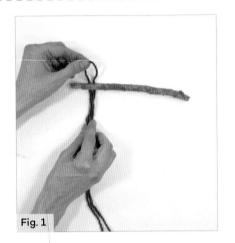

Fig. 1

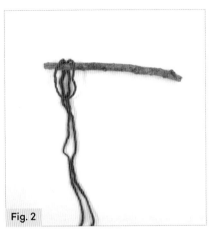

Fig. 2

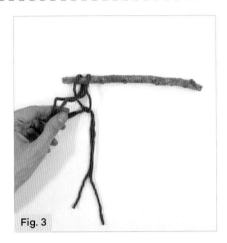

Fig. 3

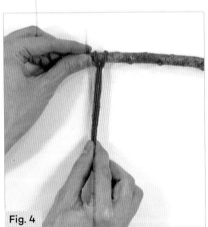

Fig. 4

Fig. 5

making a yarn tapestry

1. Find a sturdy stick. If it is very rough, sand it gently. Gather yarn in a variety of pleasing colors. Cut them into 20" (50.8 cm) strips.

2. Fold one length of yarn in half. Place the loop of yarn under the stick. **(Fig. 1)**

3. Bring the loop down over the two strands of yarn. **(Fig. 2)**

4. Pull the two strands of yarn through the loop. **(Fig. 3)**

5. Pull the ends of the yarn tightly. **(Fig. 4)**

Fig. 6

Fig. 7

Fig. 8

6. Continue this process across the length of the stick. **(Fig. 5)**

7. To trim the yarn and make it even, place a piece of tape across the yarn. Trim the ends of the yarn even with the tape. **(Fig. 6)**

8. To shape the ends of the yarn, cut the desired shape from paper and tape it over the yarn. Then cut along the edge of the paper. **(Fig. 7)**

9. Remove the tape. Add a hanger by tying a length of yarn on each side of the stick and tying it in a double knot. **(Fig. 8)**

or try this

Add pom poms to one side or both sides of the stick for added decoration. Use yarn to tie them to the stick.

(continued)

ojos de dios (god's eye)

Ojos de Dios is Spanish for "Eye of God." God's eyes were first created by the Huicol people, who are indigenous people of Mexico. The Huicol Indians created the ojos de dios to watch over those who prayed. The woven pieces are made from a cross of sticks with the four ends of the sticks representing earth, water, wind, and fire. Creating your own ojos de dios can be a lot of fun. Once you master creating them with craft sticks, try creating them from sticks found outside.

materials

→ **Craft sticks**
→ **Glue**
→ **Yarn**

making an ojos de dios

1. Place a drop of glue in the middle of a craft stick. Center another stick over the glue dot to making a lower case 'T.' Allow the glue to dry. **(Fig. 1)** Hold the connected sticks like an X. Wrap yarn over the inter-section of the X. Leave a 1" (2.5 cm) tail of yarn. Hold the yarn in place with your thumb. **(Fig. 2)**

3. Wrap the long end of the yarn directly across the X. Bring the yarn around from the back and go from the top to the bottom of the X. Re-peat one more time. **(Fig. 3)**

4. Now it is time to weave the God's eye. To do this, wrap the yarn around the sticks in this pattern: behind a stick and around. Rotate the X. Behind the next stick and around. **(Fig. 4 and Fig. 5)**

5. To complete the God's eye, cut the yarn so there is a 4" (10.2 cm) tail. Wrap the yarn loosely around the last stick. Slide the end of the yarn into the loop of yarn created and pull tight. Add a dot of white glue to hold yarn end in place. **(Fig. 6)**

variation idea: woven shell turtles

Use the same skills to make some woven turtles, but instead of craft sticks, use chenille sticks! Bend all the ends of the chenille sticks around to create the feet, head, and tail. Bend the weaving up in the middle to create the curve of the shell. Add googly eyes to finish it off!

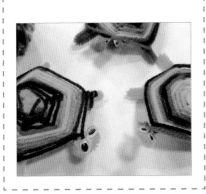

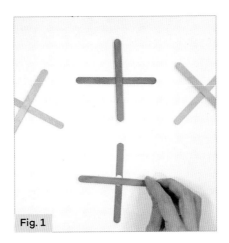

Fig. 1

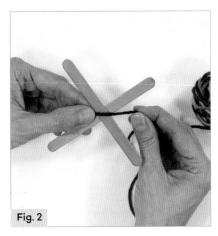

Fig. 2

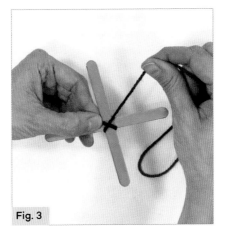

Fig. 3

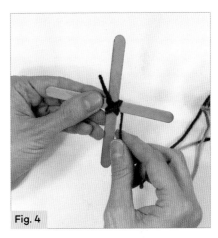

Fig. 4

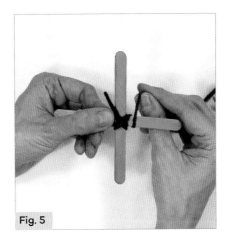

Fig. 5

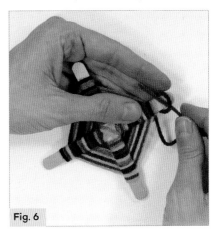

Fig. 6

string art

LAB 29

String art is sometimes called nail and thread art because it is traditionally created with pins in a wooden board and thread wrapped around the nails to create an image. For this lab, cardboard replaces the wood and a needle and thread is used to create a geometric design.

materials

→ Cardboard, 8" (20.3 cm) square
→ Paints and paintbrush, optional
→ Lid, bowl, or dish for tracing a circle
→ Thumbtack or pin
→ Marker or pencil
→ Blunt tapestry needle
→ Yarn
→ Tape

preparing for string art

1. Begin by recycling a cardboard box. Try painting the box to add color to the background of the string art design. Once dry, cut the cardboard to a square shape. In this lab, the square is 8" (20.3 cm). **(Fig. 1)**

2. On the reverse side of the cardboard square, trace a round plate or lid. The larger the circle, the bigger the ultimate design. The design here shows a 6" (15.2 cm) diameter circle on a 8" (20.3 cm) square. Draw four lines extending from the circle, representing the north, south, east and west directions. Between each of those lines, draw four more. **(Fig. 2)**

3. Between each of those lines, draw eight more for a total of sixteen evenly spaced lines extending from the circle. **(Fig. 3)**

4. At the point where each line meets the circle, use a pushpin, thumbtack, or sewing pin to make a small hole. Then push the tapestry needle through each of the small holes to enlarge them slightly.

making radiating lines string art

1. Thread the needle with yarn but do not tie a knot. Begin on the back of the cardboard where the circle is drawn. Starting at any hole, push the needle through to the front until a small yarn tail is on the back. Secure the tail with tape. **(Fig. 4)**

2. The hole where the yarn is taped is now the spot where all the yarns will radiate or come from. Pull the needle and thread through the hole until the taped back stops the thread. Insert the needle into the hole just to the right of the one where the needle came out. On the back of the cardboard, bring the needle back up through the first hole and then down again into the second hole from the radiating hole. Continue bringing the needle up through the first hole and diving down the next. **(Fig. 5)**

Fig. 1

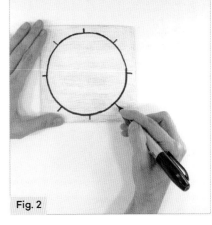

Fig. 2

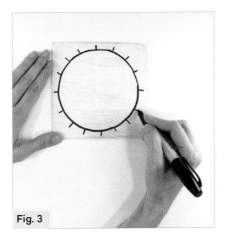

Fig. 3

Fig. 4

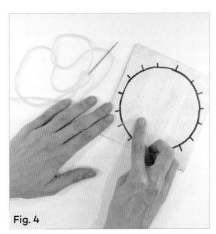

Fig. 5

(continued)

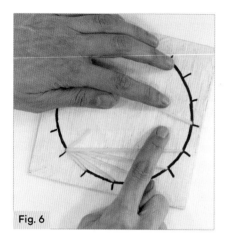

Fig. 6

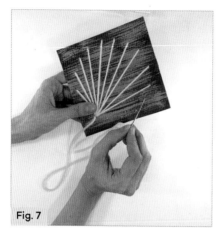

Fig. 7

Fig. 8

3. When the yarn runs out, tape the end to the back of the cardboard. Rethread the needle with new yarn, start in the back and tape the new tail of yarn. **(Fig. 6)**

4. Finish stitching from the original hole to all the other holes. **(Fig. 7)**

5. To create the illusion of a stitched sphere, pick a hole directly across from where all the first yarn lines radiated from and repeat the stitching process with a different color yarn. **(Fig. 8)**

making spectrum string art

1. To create a spectrum design, follow some of the same steps as for the radiating lines design. Start on the back, tape the yarn in place. Stitch lines that radiate from the chosen hole, however instead of stitching all the way around, only stitch six times. **(Fig. 9)**

2. After six stitches, cut the yarn and tape the tail of yarn on the back. Rethread the needle with new yarn. Now, move over just one hole to the right of the first hole. This is the new spot for the yarn to radiate from. Stitch six times. **(Fig. 10)**

3. Continue moving over a hole and stitching six times until the design is complete. **(Fig. 11)**

making tumbling square string art

1. For a tumbling square design, begin on the back and tape the tail of yarn in place. Pull the needle up through the first hole until the tape stops it. Count four holes. Have the needle dive down the fourth hole. This stitch marks the top of the square. **(Fig. 12)**

2. Count four holes, have the needle come up from the back of the fourth hole and backstitch to the end of the last line of the square. The two stitches should create an angle. Stitching the square requires a lot of yarn. If the yarn is getting short, tape the end on the back. Rethread the needle to continue.

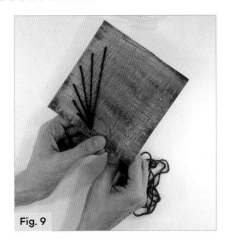

Fig. 9

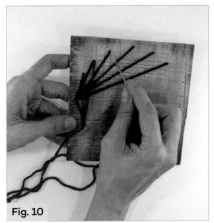

Fig. 10

Fig. 11

3. Starting on the back again, bring the yarn up from the back. Begin at the end of the lines of the square. Count four holes and bring the needle down through the fourth hole. As in step 2, count four holes and have the needle come up from the back of the fourth hole and back stitch. Now a square is created.

4. To create the tumbling block effect, stitch another square, following the same steps. This time the square begins one hole to the right or left of the last one. Four different tumbling squares fit in this design. **(Fig. 13)**

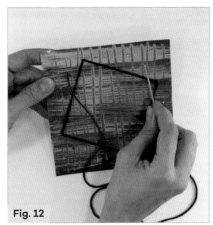

Fig. 12

Fig. 13

spool knitting

Knitting is way of looping yarn into a textile or fabric and is usually done with two knitting needles. Spool knitting is an easy and fun way to learn how to knit. In this lab, you build a simple contraption, a knitting tube for spool knitting, from craft sticks and a cardboard tube.

materials

→ Toilet paper tube
→ 4 craft sticks
→ Clear tape
→ Yarn

making a spool knitting tube

1. Tape a craft stick to the cardboard tube so that it extends about an inch above the top of the tube. **(Fig. 1)**

2. Tape another craft stick opposite the first one, in the same way. Tape the last two sticks between the first two on either side. **(Fig. 2)**

tip
If clear tape doesn't hold, try using a stronger tape or glue.

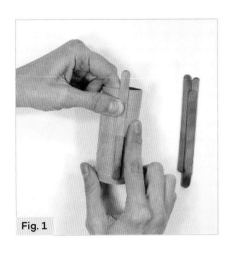

Fig. 1

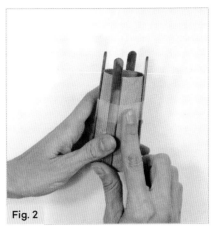

Fig. 2

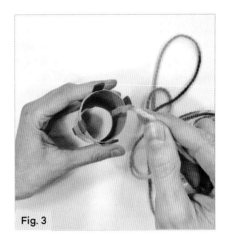

Fig. 3

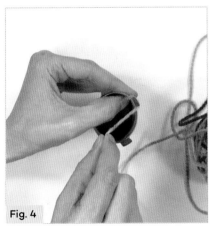

Fig. 4

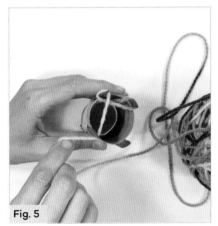

Fig. 5

Fig. 6

knitting with a spool knitting tube

1. Lower the end of the yarn into the tube until it touches the bottom. **(Fig. 3)**

2. With one hand, pinch the yarn end in place inside the tube with your thumb and wrap your fingers around the outside of the tube. With your other hand, wrap the long end of the yarn around one stick. **(Fig. 4)**

3. Move the yarn toward the stick to the left of the wrapped stick. Wrap the yarn around the stick and move the yarn toward the next stick on the left. **(Fig. 5)**

4. Go around the next stick. Continue until all four sticks have been wrapped. **(Fig. 6)**

(continued)

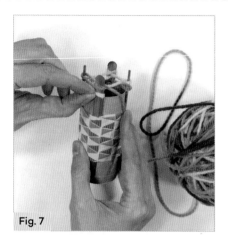
Fig. 7

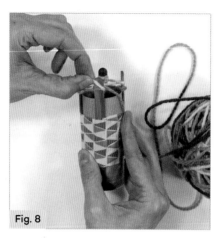
Fig. 8

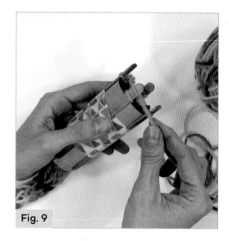
Fig. 9

Fig. 10

5. It's time to start knitting! To do that, tilt the tube. There should be two loops around one stick. Pinch the bottom loop. **(Fig. 7)**

6. Pull the loop up and over the entire stick and then let it drop inside the tube. This is knitting. **(Fig. 8)**

7. Continue this pattern of wrapping the yarn around the next stick, pinching the bottom loop, pulling it off the stick, and letting it drop inside the tube. After about five minutes, your knitted yarn should start to come out the bottom of the tube. **(Fig. 9)**

8. Once your knitted yarn is long enough to make into a belt or a headband, it is time to take it off the tube. To do this, cut the yarn at the top of the tube so it is about 6" (15.2 cm) long. Pluck all four of the loops off the end of the tube. Feed the end of the yarn through all four of the loops and pull and then knot the yarn end. **(Fig. 10)**

> **tip**
> The knitting tube can be used again and again to create more scarves or belts. Try using a variegated yarn for more color.

finger knitting

Now that you've learned the basics of spool knitting, let's try your hand, literally, at finger knitting! In this lab, the only necessary supplies are your fingers and yarn. This is a fun craft to try with extra yarn.

materials

→ **Skein or balls of thick yarn**
→ **Scissors**

learning to knit with your fingers

1. Drape an uncut strand of yarn over your open, non-dominant hand. Leave 6" (15.2 cm) long tail of the yarn around your index finger and draped behind your hand. **(Fig. 1)**

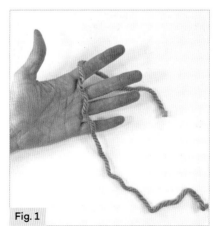

Fig. 1

(continued)

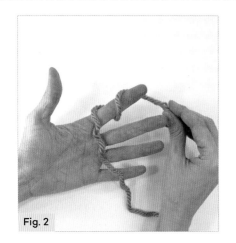
Fig. 2

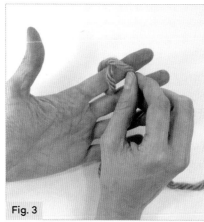
Fig. 3

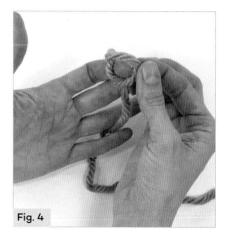
Fig. 4

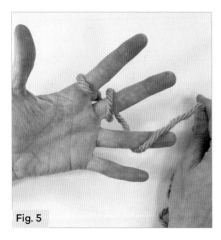
Fig. 5

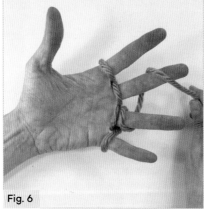
Fig. 6

anchored to your index finger with a slipknot. **(Fig. 4)**

3. With the long strand of yarn, begin loosely wrapping the yarn under and around the middle, ring, and pinkie fingers. **(Fig. 5)**

4. Bring the yarn back to the index finger by wrapping it under and over the ring, middle, and index fingers. There should be two "rings" of yarn around all your fingers except the pinkie. **(Fig. 6)**

5. Starting at your index finger, bend your finger down and pull the bottom ring of yarn to create an opening of yarn. **(Fig. 7)**

2. Tie a slipknot to anchor the yarn and begin knitting. To make a slipknot, wrap the short end of the yarn loosely around your index finger twice and let if fall behind your index finger. **(Fig. 2)**

• Bring the bottom strand over the upper strand. **(Fig. 3)**

• Then bring the bottom strand over the strand above it to create an opening. Slide your index finger into the opening between the two strands of yarn, so the yarn is

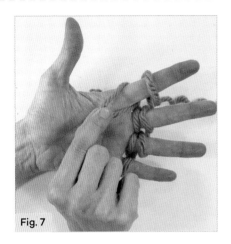

Fig. 7

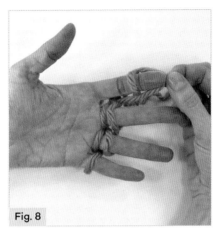

Fig. 8

Fig. 9

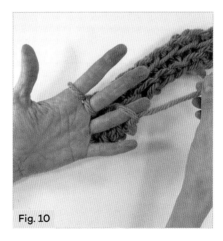

Fig. 10

6. Pull the yarn upwards and slide your index finger into the opening. **(Fig. 8)**

7. Repeat with your middle and ring fingers. Because the pinkie finger only has one ring of yarn around it, skip this finger.

8. Now each finger only has one ring of yarn. Time to add a second ring of yarn and repeat the process! The length of yarn should be behind the index finger. Bring it under and over middle, ring, and pinkie finger. This time, the index finger will only have one ring of yarn.

9. Repeat the process of bending your finger with two rings of yarn, sliding your finger into opening, and rewrapping the remaining fingers. The knitting will begin to appear behind your fingers.

10. When the knit tube is long enough, remove it by cutting the yarn, leaving a 6" (15.2 cm) long tail. **(Fig. 9)**

11. Slide the cut end of yarn into the rings of yarn on your fingers. Slide the rings of yarn off your fingers. **(Fig. 10)**

12. Slide the cut end of the yarn through all four rings once more. To tie a knot, bring the yarn into the last loop created.

wet felted fiber

Felted fiber is created with wool roving, water, and agitation. Look at the wool roving, it is made up of small strands of wool fiber. Under a microscope, these individual fibers have little barbs sticking off them. When these barbs get wet and are rubbed together, they begin to shrink and lock together. This creates a piece of felt. Felt can then be cut into different shapes without unraveling. Try making your own felted fiber to be cut out and added to gift cards or to hang as an ornament!

materials

→ Wool roving in a variety of colors
→ Zipper sealed plastic bag
→ Water
→ Foam soap
→ Scissors

working with wool roving

1. Open a zipper sealed bag. Pour three tablespoons of water into the bag. Add three pumps of foam soap. Close the bag and rub the bag with your fingertips to mix the water and soap.

2. Pull tufts of roving from a bundle, the same way you pull off bites of cotton candy. Never cut roving with scissors, always pull it. **(Fig. 1)**

3. Open the bag and put the tufts of roving into one corner of the bag. Close the bag. **(Fig. 2)**

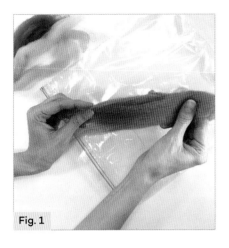

Fig. 1

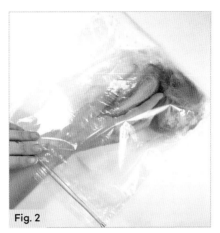

Fig. 2

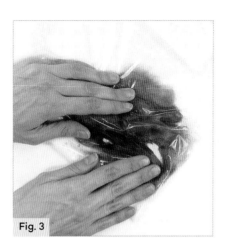

Fig. 3

4. Rub the outside of the bag with your fingertips. The soap should help the bag move easily over the roving. If the roving sticks to the bag, open it and add a small amount more of soap and water. Continue rubbing the bag for five minutes on both sides of the bag. **(Fig. 3)**

5. Open the bag and squeeze all the water out of the roving. Lay it flat on the outside of the bag and allow it to dry overnight. **(Fig. 4)**

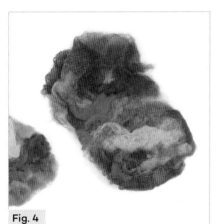

Fig. 4

Fig. 5

6. Once the newly felted piece has dried, use scissors to cut it into different shapes. Use a thread and needle to slide a string through the felt to hang the cut shape or glue it to a card and give it to a friend. **(Fig. 5)**

needle felted glitter tree

Needle felting is different than wet felting. In needle felting, there is no water. Instead, the fibers in the wool roving are locked together with a special needle felting tool. This tool is not only very sharp but also barbed. Be very careful with this tool and keep your fingers away from the needle felting cushion. In this lab, inspiration is drawn from the artist Gustauv Klimt and his painting, Tree of Life.

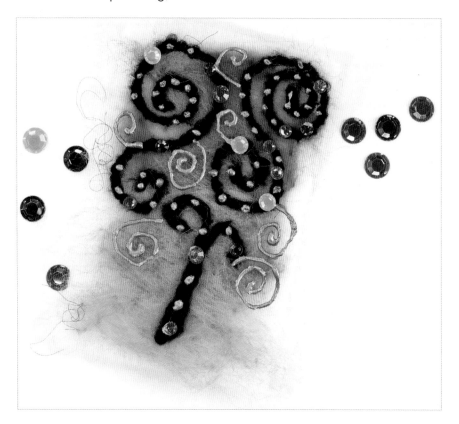

materials

→ Wool roving
→ Craft store felt
→ Yarn
→ Wooden skewer stick
→ Needle felting needle
→ Needle felting cushion
→ Gold puffy paint
→ Flat-sided gemstones, optional

making a felted glitter tree

1. Place a piece of felt onto the needle felting cushion. Gently pull small tufts of roving as if pulling cotton candy. Place the roving on the felt. **(Fig. 1)**

2. Begin to needle felt by holding the needle felting needle vertically. Use an up and down motion to poke or stab the roving. Keep your fingers out of the way! **(Fig. 2)**

3. Once a colorful background of needle felted roving is complete, place yarn over the roving, on the felt. Curve the yarn into a spiral. **(Fig. 3)**

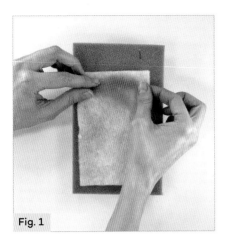

Fig. 1

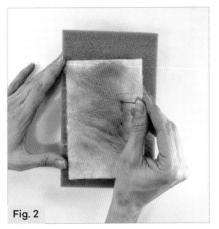

Fig. 2

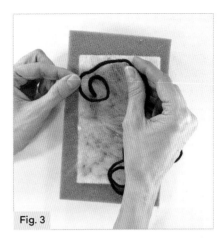

Fig. 3

Fig. 4

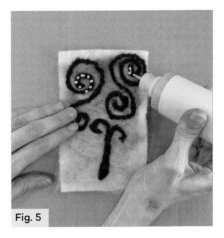

Fig. 5

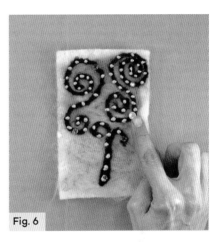

Fig. 6

4. Use the wooden skewer to hold the yarn in place. Gently stab the yarn through the felt fabric. This will tack it down and keep it in place. If you aren't happy with the design, gently pull the yarn out and try again. **(Fig. 4)**

5. Use gold puffy paint to add dots along the trunk and branches of the tree. **(Fig. 5)**

6. For added sparkle, place flat-sided gemstones onto the puffy paint while it is wet. Draw more spirals on to the design. Allow the paint to dry overnight. **(Fig. 6)**

needle felted patches

Needle felting can be done on nearly every fiber surface. This means you can needle felt designs on sweaters and jackets. In this lab, patches are designed and then stitched to a jacket. Whatever is needle felted on, must be hand washed gently otherwise the wool fibers will wet felt and shrink!

materials

→ 3" (7.6 cm) square of craft felt
→ Wool roving, various colors
→ Needle felting needle
→ Chalk (optional)
→ Yarn (does not have to be wool)
→ Wooden skewer stick
→ Foam cushion
→ Needle
→ Thread
→ Jacket, or other surface for the patches

making a pizza-shaped needle felted patch

1. Draw a simple design on a piece of craft store felt. Drawing with chalk makes it easy to brush or wipe away mistakes. **(Fig. 1)**

2. Gently pull a piece of roving, as if it were a bite of cotton candy. Never cut wool roving. **(Fig. 2)**

3. Place the felt (with the chalk design) on the foam cushion. Arrange the roving on the design. Using a cushion prevents the needle

Fig. 1

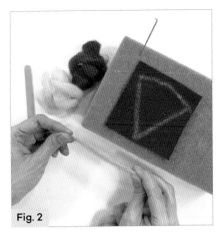

Fig. 2

Fig. 3

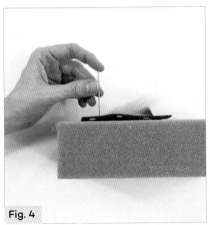

Fig. 4

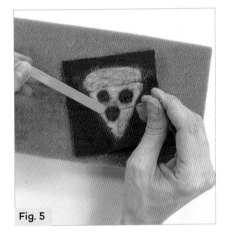

Fig. 5

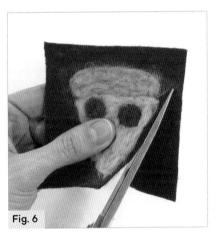

Fig. 6

from breaking during felting. Use the skewer to hold the roving in place. **(Fig. 3)**

4. To secure the roving permanently, use the needle to poke the roving down through the felt piece. This is called needle felting. Be sure to keep the needle vertical and puncture the roving and the felt fabric to lock the roving in place. If the needle bends, it will break. **(Fig. 4)**

5. Never place your fingers on the cushion while you are felting. This could cause an injury. Use the skewer to hold the roving in place. **(Fig. 5)**

6. Yarn can also be needle felted. Do not cut the yarn before felting, but do trim it after the design is complete and then felt the ends of the yarn in place. **(Fig. 6)**

(continued)

Fig. 7

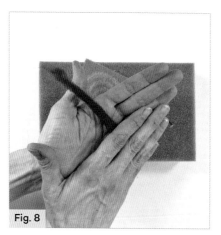

Fig. 8

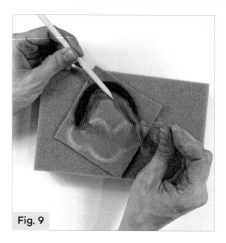

Fig. 9

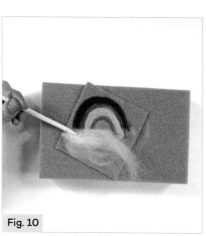

Fig. 10

7. To add small designs like dots, roll a small piece of roving between your fingers to create a small ball. Place it on the design, hold in place with a skewer, and needle felt it in place. **(Fig. 7)**

making a rainbow needle felted patch

1. For a rainbow, roll a tuft of roving in between your hands to create a snake. **(Fig. 8)**

2. Needle felt the roving into place. **(Fig. 9)**

3. Continue with the other colors. Add a tuft of white roving at the bottom for a cloud and needle felt it in place. **(Fig. 10)**

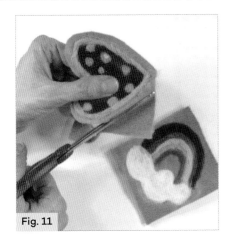

Fig. 11

Fig. 12

preparing and attaching the patches

1. Once the patches are complete, cut them out, leaving a ¼" (6.4 mm) edge around the felting. This will be where the patch is stitched to the jacket. **(Fig. 11)**

2. Thread a sharp needle, tie a knot at the end the thread, and whipstitch the patch to the jacket. **(Fig. 12)**

3. Whipstitch around the entire patch. Bring the thread to the wrong side and knot the thread securely. **(Fig. 13 and Fig. 14)**

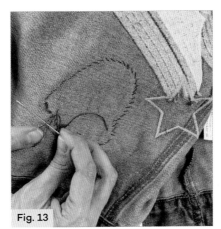

Fig. 13

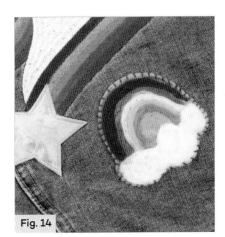

Fig. 14

LAB 35 colorful shibori

Shibori dyeing is way of folding, binding, and dying fabric traditionally in indigo, or dark blue, dye. This method comes from Japan. There are many ways to fold and bind the fabric and the fun is really in exploring different techniques. In this lab, we don't use indigo ink, instead we use permanent markers and alcohol to change the color of muslin fabric.

materials

→ **Sharpie or permanent markers**
→ **70% rubbing alcohol**
→ **Small bowl**
→ **Clothespins**
→ **Plastic bag**
→ **Muslin or t-shirt fabric cut to 8"-10" (20.3-25.4 cm) squares**

shibori dying with colorful markers

1. Fold the fabric in half lengthwise and then in half again. **(Fig. 1)**

2. Make a triangle fold at the top, as shown. Continue to fold triangles, forward and then backward, the length of the fabric. **(Fig. 2)**

3. Hold the folded fabric together with a clothespin. **(Fig. 3)**

4. Use permanent makers to color the edges of the fabric. The more color you add, the better the fabric will dye. Try letting the marker rest on the fabric and allow the ink to flow from the marker to the fabric. **(Fig. 4)**

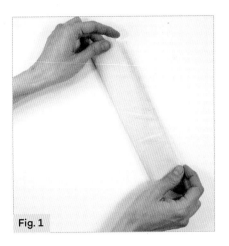

Fig. 1

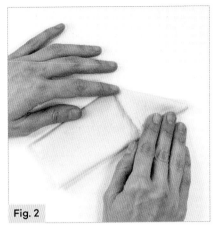

Fig. 2

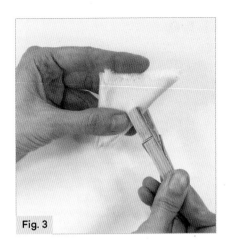

Fig. 3

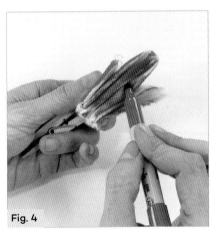

Fig. 4

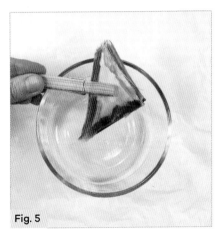

Fig. 5

Fig. 6

5. Pour rubbing alcohol in a shallow dish. Hold the fabric by the clothespin and dip it into the alcohol. Repeat for each edge of the fabric until the fabric is completely wet. **(Fig. 5)**

6. Let the fabric dry overnight on a plastic bag. Once it is completely dry, unclip, and unfold. **(Fig. 6)**

or try this
Experiment with different types of fabric folds. Think of folding the fabric like origami and adding a variety of colors for different effects. It is always a surprise to unfold shibori dyed fabric!

LAB 36 marble rolled fabric

Shopping for fabric with a print is a lot of fun...but sometimes creating an original fabric design, that no one else has, is even better. In this lab, we create a fabric that can be used for many of the sewing labs including Lab 11.

materials

→ Muslin, old t-shirt, or any type of light colored fabric
→ Tape
→ Spray bottle with water
→ Acrylic or tempera paint
→ Cardboard lid or pizza box
→ Marbles or wooden beads

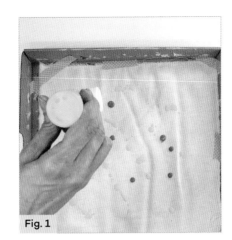
Fig. 1

creating marble rolled fabric

1. Cut the fabric to fit inside a box. Tape the corners and edges of the fabric to hold it smooth inside the box. Clean pizza boxes work well.

2. Dilute or water down the paint a bit. If the paint is applied too thickly to the fabric, it makes the fabric difficult to sew through.

3. Lightly spray the fabric with water. Add drops of paint randomly over the fabric. **(Fig. 1)**

Fig. 2

4. Drop a few marbles or wooden beads into the box. Tilt the box so the marbles roll through the paint and around the fabric.

5. Stop rolling the marbles when you are happy with the way the fabric looks. Remove the marbles and let the fabric dry. Take the fabric from the box so you can use to for all sorts of sewing projects. **(Fig. 2)**

unit
4
weaving
+
string craft

Weaving involves a lot of words that start with the letter W, including warp and weft. This can be kind of confusing, but by the end of this chapter it will all make sense. Just remember: weaving is the act of taking a fiber and going over and under other fibers. Weaving is done on a loom, and in the following labs, looms take on many different shapes and sizes from a small plate to a collection of drinking straws! Enjoy the process as you see how individual strands of fiber can be magically transformed into three-dimensional structures.

woven mat

Let's learn the basics of weaving with this simple yarn mat. We will create a loom from simple cardboard. The vertical strings will be our warp and our weaving strings, which are horizontal, will be our weft. Remember, the pattern is always over and under for weaving!

Fig. 1

materials

→ Cardboard, cut 5½" × 7"
   (12.7 × 17.8 cm)
→ Ruler or tape measure
→ Scissors
→ Pencil or marker
→ Solid color yarn for
   warping the loom
→ 2 large craft sticks
→ Yarn, cut into 8" (20.3 cm)
   lengths
→ Tape

weaving a mat with yarn

1. Use a ruler or tape measure to make a small tic mark every ½" (1.3 cm) inch along both of the shorter edges of the cardboard. There should be 10 lines at the top and 10 at the bottom. Cut those lines about ¼" (6.4 mm) long to form notches for the yarn. **(Fig. 1)**

2. Now that the loom is made, it is time to warp the loom. "To warp"

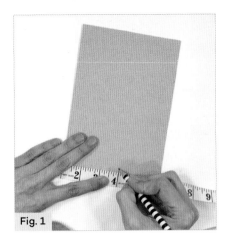

Fig. 1

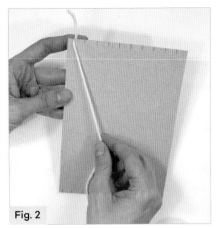

Fig. 2

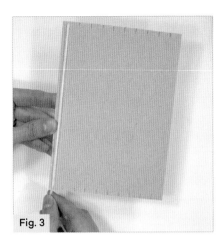

Fig. 3

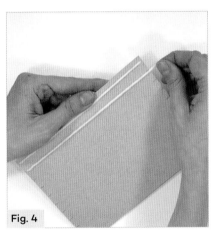

Fig. 4

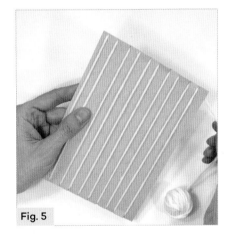

Fig. 5

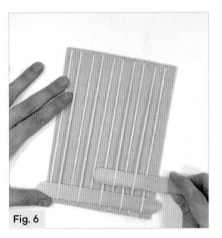

Fig. 6

means to wrap strings on the loom for weaving. To warp the loom, place the end of an uncut ball (or skein) of yarn into one of the corner notches of the loom. Leave a short tail of yarn in the back; the rest of the yarn will be in the front **(Fig. 2)**. Secure the yarn tail to the back with tape.

3. Bring the yarn directly down and slide it into the bottom notch. **(Fig. 3)**

4. Wrap the yarn around the back of the cardboard and into the next notch, so the yarn stays on the front of the cardboard. Bring the yarn directly up to the top, as shown. **(Fig. 4)**

5. Continue warping the loom until all the notches on the front are filled with yarn. It should resemble a harp. Cut the end of the yarn and tape on the back of the cardboard. There should be no harp lines on the

back, just the small lines of yarn between the notches. **(Fig. 5)**

6. Now it is time to weave. Weaving is a pattern of over and under. To practice, take a large craft stick and weave it through the loom, going over one strand of yarn and under the next. Weave the second stick in a pattern that is the opposite of the first. This is how the yarn weaving will look. **(Fig. 6)**

(continued)

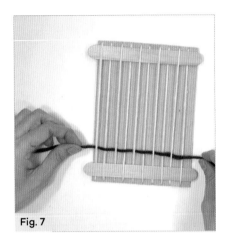

Fig. 7

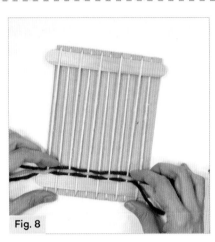

Fig. 8

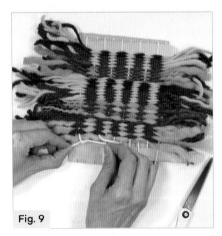

Fig. 9

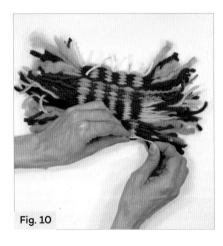

Fig. 10

7. Push one stick to the bottom and the other to the top. Pick one strand of yarn and weave the yarn through the loom in a pattern opposite of the stick. **(Fig. 7)**

8. Choose the next yarn strand and weave it opposite of the previous strand. Use your fingers to pack the yarn down toward the bottom craft stick. **(Fig. 8)**

9. When the weaving has reached the top craft stick, it is time to take it off the cardboard loom. Very carefully, slide the bottom craft stick out, two strands of warp yarn at a time. Pluck the warp yarns from the notches at one end of the loom. Cut the warp yarns so you can tie them in double knots all the way across the weaving. **(Fig. 9)**

10. Once the warp yarns are cut and knotted on one end of the loom, repeat the same process on the other end. Trim the weaving strands on the sides to even them out. **(Fig. 10)**

or try this

Instead of weaving with yarn, weave with narrow ribbon, for a totally different look.

woven basket

Weavings don't always involve weaving with yarn on a flat loom. Anything can be turned into a loom if you use your imagination! Let's try our hand at weaving a basket by using a treat bag or a cup!

materials

→ Cardboard or other sturdy treat bag or container with scalloped edge (optional)
→ Scissors
→ Tape
→ Small skein or ball of yarn for making the loom
→ Yarns for weaving, cut in different lengths
→ Ribbon, different lengths and widths (optional)

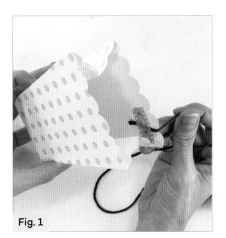

Fig. 1

making a woven basket

1. Open the cardboard treat bag. Slide the yarn into one of the scalloped notches, near a corner on the front or back, and secure the yarn inside with tape. **(Fig. 1)**

> **tip**
> If the treat bag is not scalloped across the top, you can cut an even number of ½" (1.3 cm) notches around the top edge.

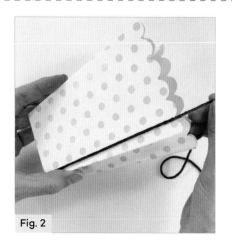

Fig. 2

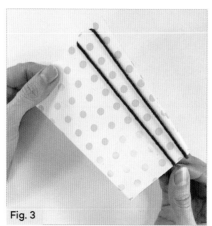

Fig. 3

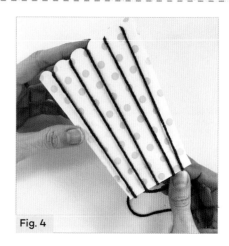

Fig. 4

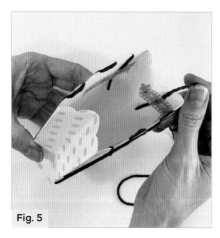

Fig. 5

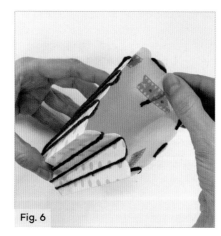

Fig. 6

2. To warp the treat bag, bring the yarn down the front, across the bottom, and up the other side. Slide the yarn directly into the notch directly opposite the first notch on the other side of the treat bag. **(Fig. 2)**

3. Slide the yarn into the next notch (on the same side) and bring the yarn to the bottom of the treat bag, across the bottom, and up the other side. **(Fig. 3)**

4. Continue warping the treat bag in this way until both the front and the back are warped. **(Fig. 4)**

5. Cut yarn and tape the end inside the treat bag. **(Fig. 5)**

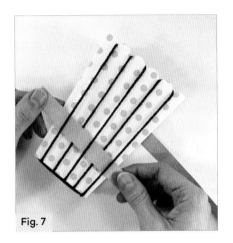
Fig. 7

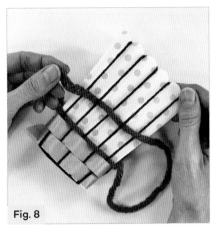
Fig. 8

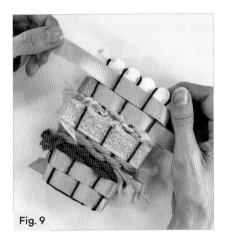
Fig. 9

6. Now it is time to warp the sides. This is done the same way as the front and back. Begin by taping the yarn on the inside of the treat bag.

7. Again, bring the yarn down and across the bottom to the opposite side, go in a notch, go out of the notch, and pull across the bottom. Continue until the sides are warped. Cut and tape the yarn on the inside of the treat bag. **(Fig. 6)**

8. Now it is time to weave, use ribbon or yarn or alternate different weaving fibers, and go over and under the warp strings. **(Fig. 7)**

9. Turn the treat bag as you weave. Be sure to always weave in the opposite pattern as the previous weft of yarn or ribbon. **(Fig. 8)**

10. To add a new weft of yarn or ribbon, just leave a short tail hanging out of the weaving. Have the new weft pick up where the last one left off. **(Fig. 9)** Weave until you reach the top of the treat bag.

or try this

You can also use a plastic drinking cup as the loom, you just need to cut an even number of ½" (1.3 cm) notches around the top edge of the cup. Follow the instructions above, but you can warp the cup with one length of thread all around the cup.

If you use a cup, continue warping the loom until all the notches are filled. Cut and tape the yarn end on the inside of the cup. Then weave the weft yarns or ribbons just like for the treat bag.

woven pouch

Let's try weaving a pouch! This lab begins like Lab 37 on page 114, because you make a cardboard loom, only this time you make a pocket of the finished project by weaving all the way around the loom.

materials

→ Cardboard, cut 4½" × 7" (11.4 × 17.8 cm)
→ Ruler or tape measure
→ Yarn or string for warping the loom
→ Yarn for weaving, cut into 12" (30 cm) lengths
→ Scissors
→ Tape
→ Tapestry needle
→ Button, optional

making a woven pouch

1. With a ruler or a tape measure, draw small lines at both the top and bottom short edges of the cardboard that are ½" (1.3 cm) apart like in Lab 37, see page 114. There should be 8 lines at the top and the bottom. Cut these notches. **(Fig. 1)**

2. Now it is time to warp the loom. Unlike in Lab 37, this loom is warped all the way around. To start, place the end of the warping string in one of the cut notches in the top corner and secure the tail with tape. Pull the string down and go into the bottom notch. **(Fig. 2)**

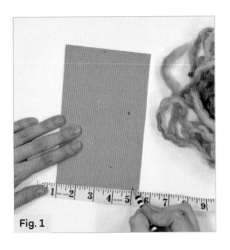

Fig. 1

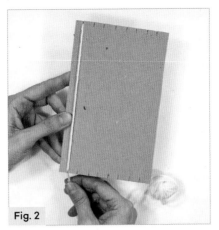

Fig. 2

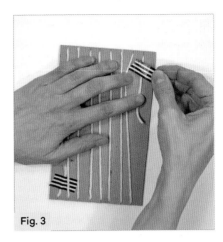

Fig. 3

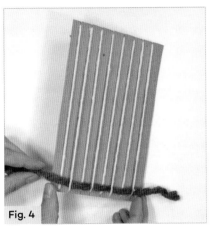

Fig. 4

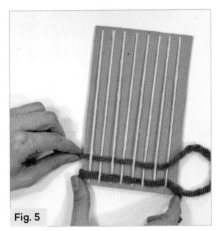

Fig. 5

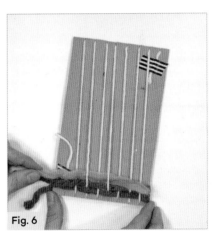

Fig. 6

3. Pull the string around the back of the cardboard, up to the top and into the next notch. Then pull the string down to the bottom and repeat. When finished, the loom looks like a harp on both the front and the back. Cut the string and secure the tail with tape. **(Fig. 3)**

4. Cut the yarn weft pieces about 12" (30 cm) long. Thread the tapestry needle with the yarn. Begin weaving at one end of the loom, passing the yarn over and under the

warp yarn. Pull the yarn until there is about a 2" (5 cm) tail hanging from the end of the loom. This thread tail is secured later. When you reach the end of the row, turn the loom over and continue weaving over and under the "back". **(Fig. 4)**

5. Once you have woven the yarn across the "back" side, turn the loom over to the front. As you continue to weave, remember to weave in the opposite pattern as the previous yarn. Over and under

the warp yarns, and then under and over the warp yarns. **(Fig. 5)**

6. Continue weaving until there is no more yarn. Thread the next length of yarn into the tapestry needle and insert the needle four warp strings back, so the yarns overlap. This secures the ends of the yarn strands in the weaving. Follow the same pattern as the last string and continue weaving. **(Fig. 6)**

(continued)

woven pouch (continued)

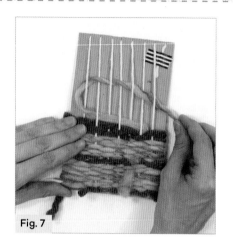
Fig. 7

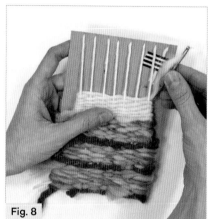
Fig. 8

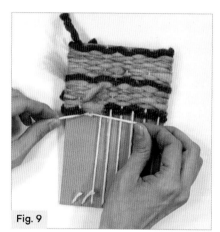
Fig. 9

7. Continue to weave around the loom, adding more yarn as needed, until the pouch is the desired height. Now it is time to weave the flap. To do this, weave only one side of the loom. Instead of turning the loom over when the yarn reaches the end of the warp strings, have the yarn loop back across the front. **(Fig. 7)**

> **tip**
> You might want to weave the flap in a different color yarn!

8. Continue weaving back and forth on the front of the loom to create the flap. When the flap has reached 2½" to 3" (6.4 × 7.6 cm), slide the needle down into the weft strings and slide the yarn off the needle. **(Fig. 8)**

9. Remove the woven pouch from the loom by cutting only two of the warp strings at a time. Begin close to the top of the loom. Double knot the first two strings on both sides of the loom. **(Fig. 9)**

10. Continue cutting two strings at a time and double knotting them on both sides of the loom. One extra string may be left. Tie it to one of the other double knotted strings. **(Fig. 10)**

11. Slide the weaving off the loom. As it comes off, it flips inside out. Leave it this way so that all the knots are now on the inside of the weaving and not visible. **(Fig. 11)**

12. If you want to be able to button the pouch closed, move the flap out of the way and sew a button onto the front of the pouch at the location covered by the flap. Be careful not to sew the button through both the front and back, or you won't be able to store things in your handwoven pouch. **(Fig. 12)**

13. Make a buttonhole in the front by separating the weft yarns on the flap and sliding the button though the opening. **(Fig. 13)**

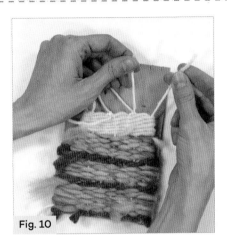

Fig. 10

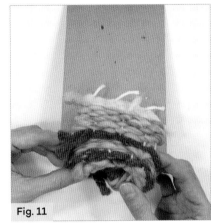

Fig. 11

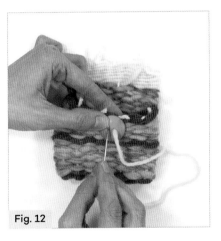

Fig. 12

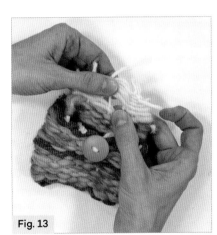

Fig. 13

circle loom weaving

Circle loom weaving is different than the past weaving labs because the loom is round. But, as with all weaving, the pattern is over and under. Keep that in mind and discover just how fun and easy circle loom weaving can be.

materials

→ Small, sturdy paper plate
→ Paint
→ Paintbrushes
→ 48" (1.2 m) length of yarn for the loom
→ Yarn for weaving
→ Ruler or tape measure
→ Scissors
→ Tape
→ Pom poms, optional

making a circle weaving

1. Every weaving is created on a loom. The loom for this weaving is a plate. To decorate the plate, paint the front before turning it into a loom. Let the paint dry. **(Fig. 1)**

2. On the back of the plate, use a tape measure or ruler to measure and mark lines every 2" (5 cm) around the rim of the plate. There should be 11 lines around the edge of the plate. Cut the lines. **(Fig. 2)**

tip

I used an 8" (20.3 cm) diameter plate, but any size works as long as you cut 11 notches around the rim or edge of the plate.

3. On the back of the plate, slide the 48" (1.2 m) of yarn into any one of the cut notches. Leave a short tale and tape it in place. On the front of the plate, take the long strand of yarn. Pull it gently down and slide into a notch at the bottom of the plate, opposite the beginning notch. **(Fig. 3)**

4. Count the empty notches on either side of the plate. Whatever side has more notches, is the one the yarn goes to next. From behind, slide it into the next closest notch and pull the yarn to the front. **(Fig 4.)**

5. Take the string to the top of the loom and slide into the notch beside the top one. This should form a narrow X on the loom. **(Fig. 5)**

6. Once again, take the string and go from the back to the front of the notch directly beside the last notch. Take the string to the opposite side of the loom. **(Fig. 6)**

(continued)

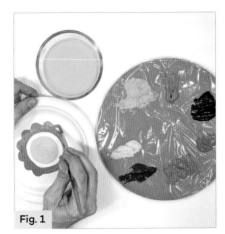

Fig. 1

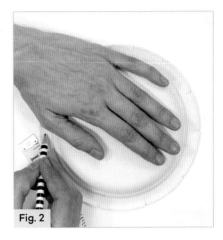

Fig. 2

Fig. 3

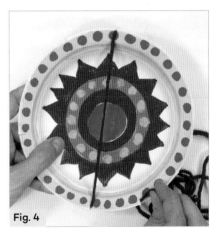

Fig. 4

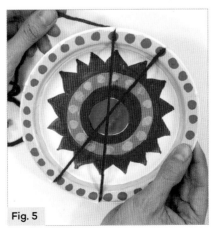

Fig. 5

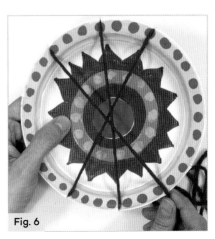

Fig. 6

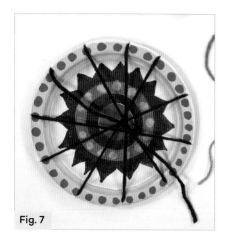
Fig. 7

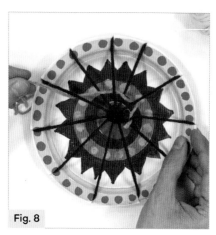
Fig. 8

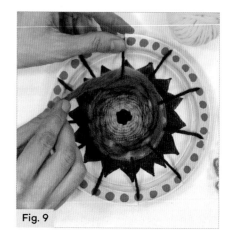
Fig. 9

7. Continue this pattern until the yarn looks like the spokes of a bicycle. There should be no empty notches. This yarn is now your loam yarn, or warp. **(Fig. 7)**

> **tip**
> If you want to vary the yarn color of the weft (loom) yarns, simply cut the first yarn and tie a new color yarn to the cut end with an overhand knot.

8. Now that the loom is made, weave different color yarns, in a circle, with the same under and over pattern. Begin by placing the weaving yarn under one of the spokes. Then go over the next. Do this pattern of under and over all the way around the plate. Pull the weaving yarns tightly. **(Fig. 8)**

9. Continue adding more yarn and weaving until your weaving is as wide as desired. Cut the yarn. Tie the end to one of the spokes of the weaving. **(Fig. 9)**

10. Tape a yarn hanger to the back and add pom poms to the bottom for decoration.

LAB 41 picture frame weaving

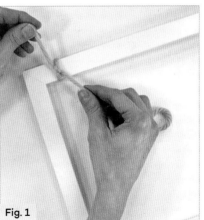

Fig. 1

materials

→ Empty picture frame
→ Skein of yarn for warping the loom
→ Yarn for weaving
→ Tapestry needle
→ Ribbon, feathers, strips of paper (optional)
→ Scissors

Like the weavings created on the round plate looms, this weaving remains on the picture frame. In this lab, you learn how to add more texture to weavings with the introduction of the rya knot.

weaving a fiber arts picture frame

1. The frame can be oriented vertically or horizontally. At the top of the frame, tie a double knot with a skein of yarn. **(Fig. 1)**

(continued)

picture frame weaving (continued)

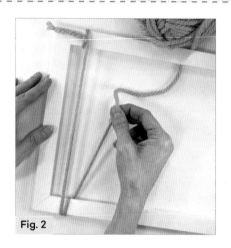

Fig. 2

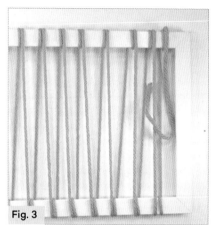

Fig. 3

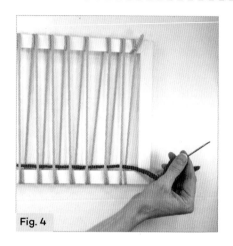

Fig. 4

2. Bring the yarn down to the bottom of the frame. Wrap it around the frame twice, going over the frame, around the frame, and then pull the yarn up towards the top. **(Fig. 2)**

3. At the top of the frame, wrap the yarn around it twice. This time, instead of going over the frame to start wrapping, begin by going under the frame, around twice, and then pull the yarn toward the bottom. Continue this pattern of wrapping the yarn twice around the frame, both at the top and the bottom. Stop wrapping on the same end of the frame as you started. **(Fig. 3)**

4. Weave over and under the warp strands with the weft yarn. Use your fingers or thread the yarn through a tapestry needle. **(Fig. 4)**

5. After weaving one row, have the yarn make a "u-turn" and begin weaving back across. This time, weave the opposite pattern. Meaning, if the last strand was under the warp string, the weft strand will go over. Continue weaving back and forth across the loom in this manner. **(Fig. 5)**

tip

For a tight weaving, warp the loom with the yarn strands close together. For a loose weaving, space the yarn strands apart. There should be an odd number of yarn strands on the loom.

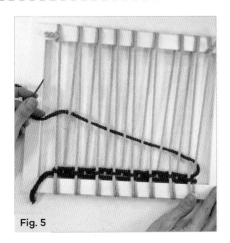

Fig. 5

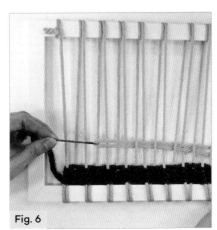

Fig. 6

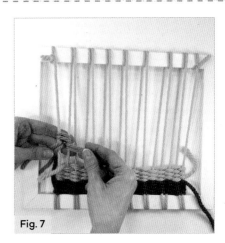

Fig. 7

6. If the yarn strand is getting short or you want to change colors, cut the original yarn, with a short tail, at one side of the weaving. Rethread the needle with a new color and pick up weaving where the last strand of yarn left off. Be certain to do the opposite pattern of weaving. Weave these thread tails back into the project with a tapestry needle once you finish the entire weaving. **(Fig. 6)**

7. To add rya knots, cut strands of yarn that are about 6" (15.2 cm) long. Hold two strands together, place the middle of the two strands of yarn over two warp strings. Pull the ends of the cut yarn between the middle of the two warp strings. **(Fig. 7)** Complete a row of rya knots in this way.

8. To complete the weaving, continue adding yarn, feathers, ribbon, or even scraps of paper to the weaving. **(Fig. 8)**

9. Weave until you reach the top of the frame. Weave any thread tails back into the project with the tapestry needle. Leave the weaving on the frame loom and hang!

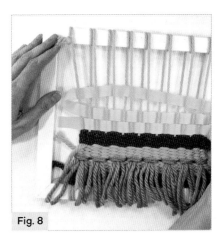

Fig. 8

tip
When weaving back and forth across a loom, pull the weft yarn gently or your weaving will begin to draw in like an hourglass.

tree weaving

This lab uses a round loom just like in Lab 40, page 124. This time, the warping is done a bit differently to create a tree weaving! Once completed, think of other things your weaving could be besides a tree—could you invert the weaving to make an evergreen tree? Could you use different colors to weave a turkey or a peacock? So many possibilities!

materials

→ Chinet plate, any size
→ Paint
→ Scissors
→ Brown yarn for the tree (loom)
→ Tape
→ Yarn for weaving
→ Tapestry needle
→ Buttons (optional)

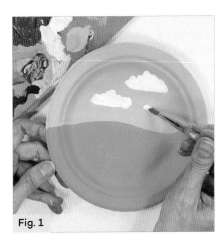

Fig. 1

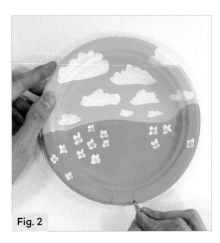

Fig. 2

weaving a tree shape

1. Paint a landscape on the right side of the plate. Pick a day or nighttime color for the sky. Paint the ground a different color, perhaps green for grass. Add details like clouds in the sky or flowers on the ground. **(Fig. 1)**

2. Once the plate is dry, decide where the tree will go. Draw two lines about a ½" (1.3 cm) apart at the bottom of the plate to indicate the tree trunk. **(Fig. 2)**

3. At the top of the plate, draw eight lines, 1" (2.5 cm) apart to indicate the top of the tree. Cut each of the drawn lines from the edge to the rim of the plate. This is your loom. The warp yarns won't go around the plate, they will go in and out of the notches, so there is minimal yarn on the back of the plate. **(Fig. 3)**

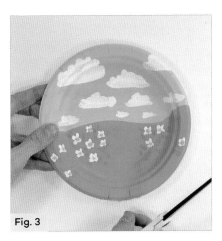

Fig. 3

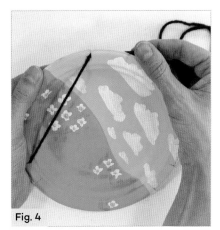

Fig. 4

4. To warp the loom, slide the end of the brown yarn into the bottom left notch. Tape the yarn tail on the back of the plate. Bring the yarn up to the top of the loom and go into the first notch on the left. **(Fig. 4)**

(continued)

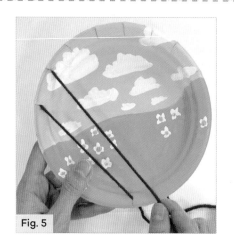

Fig. 5

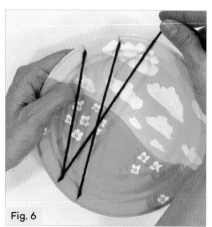

Fig. 6

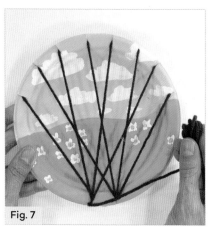

Fig. 7

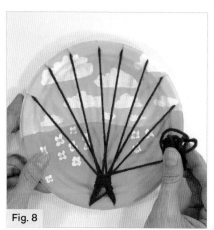

Fig. 8

5. Slide the yarn, from the back to the front, and into the notch beside the one just entered. Bring the yarn to the bottom of the plate and into the notch to the right of the first notch. **(Fig. 5)**

6. Wrap the yarn around the notch so it comes back out the original and first notch. Bring the yarn up to the top of the plate, third notch from the left and then down to right side notch on the bottom of the plate. **(Fig. 6)**

7. Continue sliding the yarn from the first notch on the bottom left into all the notches at the top and from all the top notches down to the bottom right side notch, until all the notches at the top are full and the yarn is at the bottom of the plate. **(Fig. 7)**

8. Cut the end of the yarn, leaving about 12" (30 cm) to create the trunk of the tree. Wrap the 12" (30 cm) tail over all the warp strings and then under all the warp strings. Pull the yarn tightly to bring the strings together to create the trunk. **(Fig. 8)**

9. When the trunk is the desired height, double knot the end of the yarn to one of the tree "branches."

10. Time to weave! Begin at the bottom of the tree and weave in an over and under pattern through the tree branches. **(Fig. 9)**

11. Leave a tail of yarn about 2" (5 cm) long. Start a new strand of yarn, leaving a 2" (5 cm) thread tail and continue weaving, over and under, until you reach the rim of the plate. Once you are finished weaving, use a tapestry needle to weave the thread tails into the project. **(Fig. 10)**

12. To finish, tie the last yarn to one of the warp tree branches. You can even sew or glue buttons on the tree for flowers or fruit. **(Fig. 11)**

or try this

Make an evergreen tree, by warping and weaving with two notches at the top and the eight at the bottom. Begin weaving at the top of the tree, adding the wrapped trunk last.

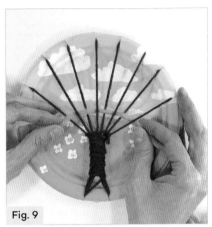
Fig. 9

Fig. 10

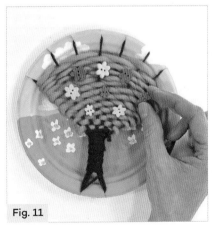
Fig. 11

straw weaving

Remember, a loom for weaving can be made from just about anything...including drinking straws! When complete, a straw weaving can use used as a bookmark, a belt, or even a wristband. Just vary the length of the warp string to alter the length of the weaving.

materials

→ 4 strands of yarn cut into 12" (30 cm) lengths
→ Tape
→ Scissors
→ 2 smoothie straws
→ Ball or skein of yarn for weaving; variegated yarn works great
→ Tapestry needle

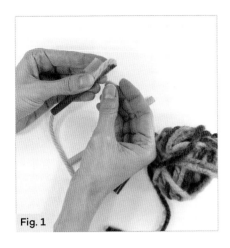

Fig. 1

Fig. 2

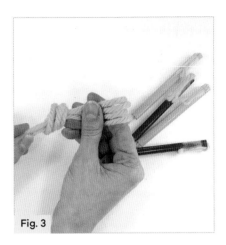

Fig. 3

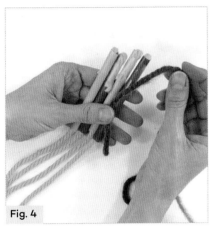

Fig. 4

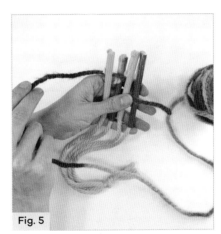

Fig. 5

weaving with straws

1. Cut two straws in half. **(Fig. 1)**

2. Tilt one of the straws down, slide one 12" (30 cm) length of yarn into the straw until just a little of the yarn comes out the end. **(Fig. 2)**

3. Secure the yarn end with tape. Repeat for the remaining three straws. **(Fig. 3)**

4. Align all the straws together at the top. Tie the bottom of the yarns together in an overhand knot. **(Fig. 4)**

5. Hold the straws together near the top with your thumb in front and fingers in back. Place the end of the weaving yarn under your thumb. Think of the straws as having a number, from left to right: 1, 2, 3, 4. **(Fig. 5)**

(continued)

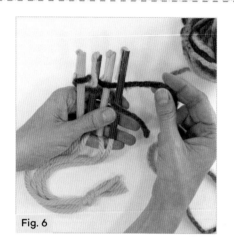

Fig. 6

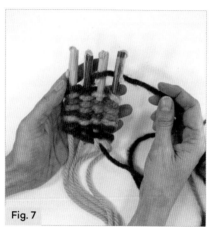

Fig. 7

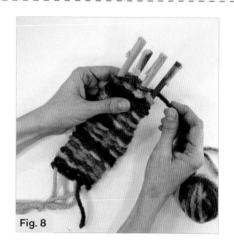

Fig. 8

Fig. 9

Fig. 10

6. Continue to hold the yarn in place with your thumb.

- With your extra hand, wrap the yarn around the back of straw 3. **(Fig. 5)**
- Then weave the yarn in front of straw 2. **(Fig. 7)**
- Loop the yarn around straw 1. **(Fig. 8)**
- Now go behind straw 2 and in front of straw 3, the opposite of the previous pattern. **(Fig. 9)**
- Loop around straw 4 and behind straw 3. Continue this weaving pattern of over, under, and around. **(Fig. 10)**

Fig. 11

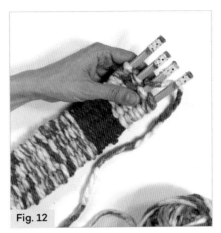
Fig. 12

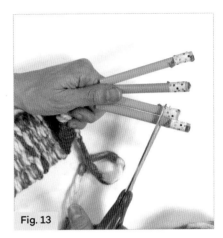
Fig. 13

7. Continue weaving. The yarn at the bottom may start to unravel a bit but don't worry about that. As the weaving grows, slowly and gently scoot it down the straws. Do not push it all the way off the straws. **(Fig. 11)**

8. When the weaving has moved all the way to the bottom of the knot and 2" (5 cm) from the top of the straws, stop. **(Fig. 12)**

9. Slide the weaving down the straws. Pinch the straws so that the yarn stays in place. Cut off the top of the straws below the tape. **(Fig. 13)**

10. Hold onto yarn so that it does not slide down the weaving and cause it to unravel. Remove the straws. **(Fig. 14)**

11. Cut the weaving (weft) yarn, leaving a 2" (5 cm) tail. Then cut a short piece of the same yarn and use it to secure the top of the weaving with an overhand knot. Use a tapestry needle to bury the beginning and end of the weft yarn thread tails. Trim the warp yarns. **(Fig. 15)**

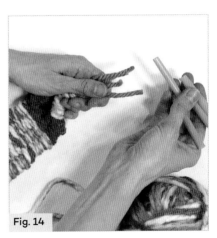
Fig. 14

kumihimo

Kumihimo is a Japanese form of braided cord making. In Japanese, kumi-himo means "gathered threads." Historically, these braided cords were used by the samurai to lace their armor. Creating these cords is highly addictive! Use them as bracelets, belts, or bookmarks.

materials

→ Cardboard, 7" (17.8 cm) square or larger
→ Pen or pencil
→ Large lid or jar for tracing, 6" (15.2 cm) in diameter or larger
→ Scissors
→ 4 strands of 18" (45.7 cm) yarn in one color
→ 4 strands of 18" (45.7 cm) yarn in a different color

weaving kumihimo

1. To create a loom, trace a round jar or a lid that is no smaller than 6" (15.2 cm) in diameter. Cut out the cardboard along the tracing. **(Fig. 1)**

2. Starting at the top of the circle, draw a short line. If this were a compass, this would be north. Draw three more lines for south, east and west. **(Fig. 2)**

3. Draw four more lines, each in the middle of the first four drawn lines. If this were a compass, these would be north-east, north-west, south-east, south-west. **(Fig. 3)**

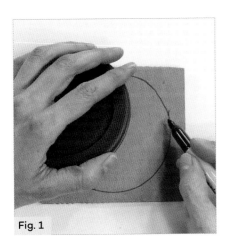

Fig. 1

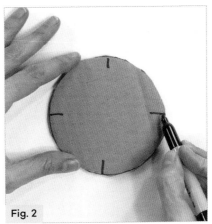

Fig. 2

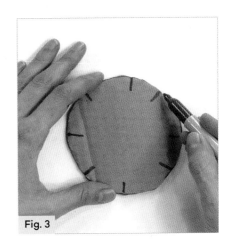

Fig. 3

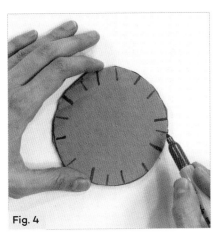

Fig. 4

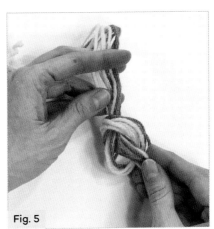

Fig. 5

Fig. 6

4. Draw a line in the middle of each of the 8 lines already drawn on the circle for a total of 16 lines on the circle. Cut about ½" (1.3 cm) into the circle on each of these lines. Use an ink pen to poke a hole into the center of the circle. **(Fig. 4)**

5. Tie the eight strands of yarn into an overhand knot at one end.
- Begin by bringing all eight strands into the shape of the letter U. **(Fig. 5)**
- Bring the short set of strands over the long strands. Place them through the loop of yarn and pull tightly. **(Fig. 6)**

(continued)

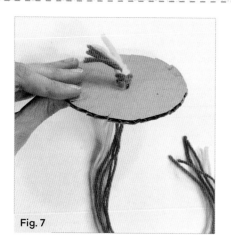

Fig. 7

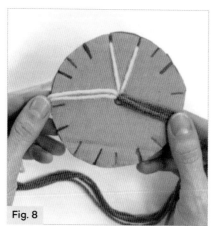

Fig. 8

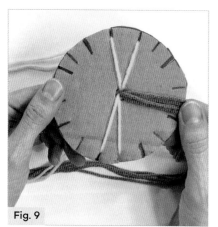

Fig. 9

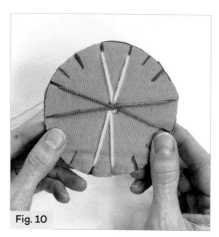

Fig. 10

6. Push the knot through the hole in the middle of the circle. **(Fig. 7)**

7. Pull the short strands of yarn through one side and leave the long on the other side. The side with the short strands is the back. Turn the loom over to the side with the long strands of yarn. This is the front and where the weaving will be done. **(Fig. 8)**

8. Separate the long strands by color. Slide one of the four strands of one color into any of the notches on the loom. Place the second strand of the same color right beside the first, creating a V. **(Fig. 9)**

9. Take the two remaining strands of the first color and slide them into two notches on the opposite end of the loom. The yarn placed in the loom should look like a very narrow X. If this were a compass, the yarn placed in the loom would be north and south. **(Fig. 10)**

10. With the four strands of yarn of the second color, follow the same steps. These strands will go in the east and west position of the imaginary compass. **(Fig. 11)**

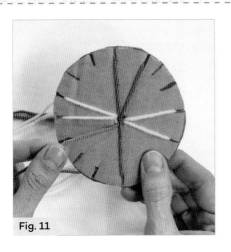
Fig. 11

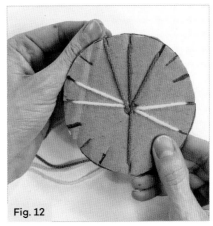
Fig. 12

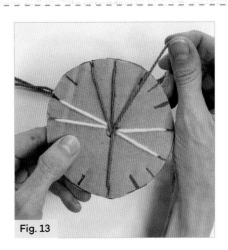
Fig. 13

11. Now for the weaving process. Once the process is learned, it is very easy. Always hold the loom in your right hand. There are two X's on the loom. One is vertical, the other horizontal. While weaving, only the X that is vertical is used. Always start at the bottom of the X, lifting the left side of the X out of the loom. **(Fig. 12)**

12. Bring that strand of yarn to the top of the X. Slide it into the loom on the top left side of the X, creating a fork. **(Fig. 13)**

13. Switch and hold the loom with your left hand, rotating the loom so the other X (the second color) is vertical. Use your right hand to remove the top right strand of the fork. **(Fig. 14)**

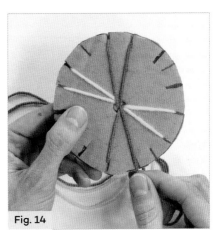
Fig. 14

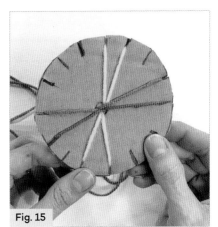
Fig. 15

14. Still using your right hand, slide the yarn into the notch on the right side of the bottom, creating an X. **(Fig. 15)**

(continued)

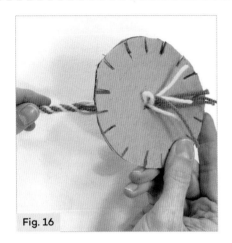

Fig. 16

Fig. 17

Fig. 18

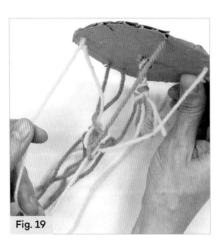

Fig. 19

15. Turn the entire loom clockwise until the X that was previously horizontal is now vertical. **(Fig. 16)** This is where steps 10-14 are repeated. To remember the steps, think of this simple poem:

Left strand to the top, right side drops, turn it like the hands of a clock.

16. While weaving, gently tug on the cord to help pull the weaving out. After about five minutes, a woven cord should be forming through the bottom of the loom **(Fig. 17)**

17. If you are uncertain which color should be woven next, look closely at the yarn. Whichever color is on top is the one that was just woven. Move on to the next color. **(Fig. 18)**

tip
It is best to leave the weaving in a fork formation when taking a break. Then it is easy to see where the weaving left off and what color to start back with.

18. If the strands of yarn may start to tangle, untangle them by pulling only one strand of yarn out of the tangle at a time **(Fig. 19)**

19. Continue weaving until the unwoven strands of yarn are no longer long enough to fit into the notches of the loom. **(Fig. 20)**

20. Take the unwoven yarn out of the loom and slide it through the hole. **(Fig. 21)**

21. At this point, the cord weaving is complete. Cut off the starting knot and the extra stands of yarn on the finished end. Leave the woven cord aa bookmark or a loop for a future weaving project. To create a bracelet, thread a chenille needle and knot one end of the yarn. Overlap the ends of the cord. Pull needle through both the bottom and the top of the cord. **(Fig. 22)**

22. Wrap the yarn around and around the two overlapped cords. Finish by stitching a knot at the end. **(Fig. 23)**

Fig. 20

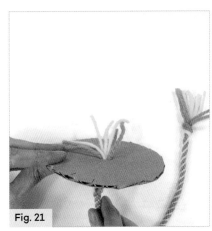
Fig. 21

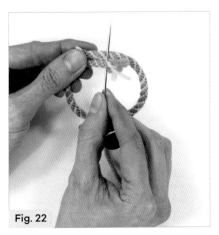
Fig. 22

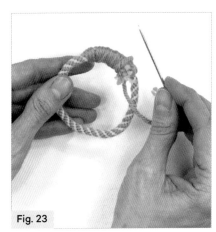
Fig. 23

tip
Hold onto the cardboard loom, it can be reused to create more cords unless it is too bent out of shape.